The Celestial Speed-Up

The Apocalypse & The End of Time

R. Lane Plaster

Order this book online at www.trafford.com
or email orders@trafford.com

Most Trafford titles are also available at major online book retailers.

Printed in the United States of America.

ISBN: 978-1-4251-0563-1 (sc)

Trafford rev. 04/11/2011

 www.trafford.com

North America & international
toll-free: 1 888 232 4444 (USA & Canada)
phone: 250 383 6864 ♦ fax: 812 355 4082

Front Cover: Halley's Comet

The Celestial Speed-Up

The Apocalypse & The End of Time

R. Lane Plaster

Table of Contents

The Second Coming of the Christ

The coming of the Christ (Self) is imminent ... One way or another, the world is going to be made a single whole entity ... it will be unified either in mutual mass destruction or ... mutual human consciousness. If a sufficient number of individuals can ... experience...the coming of the Self (Christ consciousness), we may ... be spared the worst features of ... manifesting the Apocalypse ... in its most extreme forms."

Edward Edinger, MD, *"Archetype of the Apocalypse"*

Note: Dr. Edinger (1926-1998) was considered America's dean of Jungian Psychology during his professional career and has written extensively on religious symbolism and the unconscious. His colleagues say he was the most influential Jungian analyst from the 1950's until his death. Dr. Edinger believed that many neuroses were associated with the decline of religion and the dominance of science. He thought it was important for the afflicted to grasp elements of religion, philosophy, literature and even alchemy to heal and thrive.

Acknowledgements

Several individuals have given considerable time to edit and format this book bringing it into fruition. I want to thank Keith, a study companion and final reviewer, Ed for his editing and literary assistance and Barbara, Steve, and Gwynne, all fellow students, who assisted also in editing and formatting content in an orderly fashion. And Midge Tom who made the final edits.

Thanks to Gerard who gave me a digital copy of *"A Course in Miracles"* (Hugh Lynn Cayce Edition) and to my fellow students in Dallas, Texas who taught lessons necessary to complete my writing. In particular, the Tuesday night group at Unity Church where we identified the healing rhythms of reading and questioning which unfolded the miracles received in our "Circle of Forgiveness."

Thanks to the Sunday morning Study Group whose patience and knowledge unlocked the riddle of the Book of Revelation and revealing a new meaning as viewed with Eyes of the Spirit and readings from *"A Course in Miracles."* It was their sage advice and wisdom that prompted me to explore this concept and bring it to the attention of others who may have an interest in what *"A Course in Miracles"* has to say about the key factors in the Myth of Apocalypse and the End of Time. Thanks to you all.

Dedication:

To my parents: your inspiration was invaluable in so many ways.

Purpose & Introduction

"A Universal Theology is not possible
But a universal experience is not only possible,
but necessary."
This is the Celestial Speed-Up.

"A Course in Miracles"

Why We Must Rethink the Book of Revelation

We need a new way to look at the Book of Revelation. Fortunately, one has been given. This book is a "time saving" device for those seeking a new understanding of the Apocalyptic Myth and The End of Time. It is based on teachings from *"A Course in Miracles"* but more specifically on an unpublished manuscript given to Edgar Cayce's Library. This edition contains terms and concepts of great import in rethinking our Myth of the Apocalypse. From this new perspective, there are no tales of death and destruction or any horrific end of time. By redefining its purpose, the Book of Revelation releases its grip of grief and suffering on humankind. This plague on Western minds, a torment for more than 2,000 years, is coming to an end. Hastening that end, we will experience a rapid expansion of spiritual knowledge, in the minds of a few, followed by a transfer and awareness of spiritual knowledge into our universal collective consciousness. Expanding at an accelerated rate, it will heal the minds of many. As a continuous stream of miracles, this quickening in the Spirit is the purpose of the Celestial Speed-Up.

Recent opinion polls from popular news magazines indicate more than 60 percent of Americans choose a literal belief in the Book of Revelation. These inerrant beliefs become a prescription for wars and chaos under a holy commission to fight evil. Fears engendered by this apocalyptic thinking are reflective of an intense craving for certainty and assurance. We must reconsider this choice for fear and seek a new perspective on "end times" scenarios that generated terror. A change is needed. We have an intelligent facility for change in our unconscious mind. It is the focal point of The Book of Revelation. Understood by enlightened minds for centuries, this perspective provides a pathway to awakening a higher level of spiritual understanding in every man, woman and child. This is the message of our Myth of the Apocalypse.

"A Course in Miracles" (ACIM) has the same purpose. Forgiveness is the means of awakening this greater spiritual understanding. This is not forgiveness as in a pardon. Rather, it is an admission of our misperceptions about each other. This key unlocks a process connecting desire to realization. Traveling such a path is more than a means; it is an end unto itself. This way is paved with personal meaning and fulfillment. We no longer need pursue passions outside ourselves, chasing endless forms and appearances for answers.

Get a Hold of Your Self

Dr. Carl G. Jung gave a name to this universal intelligent facility in all of us. He called this agent for order and change the Self. According to Jung it is the central and ordering archetypical energy of our conscious and unconscious minds. It is their whole circumference, as well. As an archetype of wholeness, its transpersonal power transcends our egos. In this context, the ego is the center of our conscious mind and is referred to as the "smaller self." As a speck is to the universe, so the ego is to the Self.

Archetypical images are patterns of thought and behavior that are common to mankind, at all times and in all places. The greater Self, as an archetypical image, is a transcendental concept that presupposes our unconscious mind where the archetypical energy resides. Jung suggested this analogy: if the Self is the mover, the ego is the one moved.

The greater Self is both individualized and collective. Jung's theory of a "collective mind" suggested we have a universal thought system in which everyone participates. This controversial concept, the collective mind in the unconscious, is that aspect of our collective unconscious that manifests inherited, universal themes that run through all human life. As primordial images, they reflect the basic patterns common to each of us that have existed universally since the dawn of time. We experience this archetypical energy in our conscious minds as dreams and in our imaginations, visions and instincts.

A process brings us into partial but conscious awareness of our greater Self. Jung named the process for initiating this change and then awakening "individuation." This is when we become whole or indivisible. Our "true Self" is experienced through individuation, a process of integrating the many aspects of our conscious and unconscious personality. The entire essence of the Self is unknowable, but its manifestations in our personal lives carry the greater meaning which we *seek*. Words lack in explaining this mystery.

Jung's definitions and processes are similar to those detailed in *"ACIM."* Each gives a description of how we become conscious of a new understanding of our Self. This is not something we acquire through effort or merit; this is knowledge we already have in our unconscious mind seeking to come into our conscious awareness. Its pathway is a gift of grace from our Universal Divinity. Traveling this path toward its end will result in a new understanding of our spirituality, as foretold by the Apocalyptic Myth. This is the process of *Self*-realization or individuation.

In this context, Self-realization also relates to Hindu religion referring to a profound spiritual awakening from the illusory self identified image created by our ego. What emerges is the true, divine and perfect condition that each individual will become. The Hindu sub-school of *Advaita Vedanta* fosters this concept. Noted psychologist Abraham Maslow, has defined the concept (he used the term "self-actualization") as the "impulse to convert oneself into what one is capable of being." The terms of Self-realization, self-actualization and individuation, while used interchangcably in this work, should be thought of as complementing each other rather than as equating concepts. They are but aspects of a many sided whole which we seek to understand. In the meantime, it is seeking to come into our conscious awareness. That which we seek is seeking us.

The "Archetype of the Apocalypse" and the "Celestial Speed-Up"

"ACIM" uses apocalyptic term from the Book of Revelation to describe our awakening to this higher spiritual identity, the Self. Our ego's fear of initiating this process creates turmoil and terror in individual thoughts. Manifested in the "collective unconscious mind," they become a source of chaos in our external world. As we experience these fears, we project them onto an outer source, blame follows. This

mental constellation of fear, angst and terror which resists the coming of individuation or Self-realization may be thought of as the "Archetype of the Apocalypse."

This Archetype of the Apocalypse is a powerful transpersonal energy in our collective unconscious. It is laden with affect and seething to release. It can and does possess individuals and groups to the point of self-destruction. Consider the 1992 siege in Waco, Texas where an entire religious community was engulfed in a flaming inferno or the mass suicide at Rev. Jim Jones' Jonestown that claimed the lives of more than 900 cult members. Possession is fatal for individuals, but for cultures it becomes apocalyptic: catastrophe follows. When fixated in the grip of this transpersonal energy, inhumanity has no limits. This fixation creates anomie: wars, famine, blight and disease. This need not be.

Jung was asked during World War II if he thought we, as a culture, would survive the holocaust of death and destruction then underway. He responded, "Yes, if enough of us do our inner work." The focus of this inner work he referred to was individuation or Self-realization. We each have the capacity to attain this awareness with the development of a personal relationship with our highest Divinity: the Christ or Self within. Self-realization leads us to our ultimate potential through integration of this greater Self into our conscious awareness.

Forgiveness is the method prescribed by *"ACIM"* for awakening our greater Self. In this context, forgiveness is an understanding we are not just bodies and minds, but eternal spirits. Seeking an awareness of Christ consciousness, or our higher spiritual Self, is the first step. Seeing with "Christ-vision" is the next. Forgiveness bridges a tiny gap between the perceptions of our ego and our true identity. Its reflection displays the beauty of the face of Christ within each living human being. Forgiveness looks past bodies, this is how it heals.

Forgiveness Awakens the Christ-Within

I will use the term Christ or Christ-Self as a name given by *"ACIM"* to this inner Central Archetype which is the core being of every man, woman and child. In this context, the term Christ follows the Greek definition of the "anointed one." You may think of this as the individuated and enlightened thought of God in our mind. Jesus of

Nazareth was an individual who attained this Christ awareness with such magnitude that he awakened the entire Western world to a new spiritual teaching. According to *"ACIM,"* Jesus saw the face of Christ in all of his brothers and *remembered* God; being one with God, he was a man no longer. It awaits our recognition. This is "Christ in you, the hope of glory," from St. Paul's Epistle to the Colossians.

Forgiveness is the remedy for our misperceptions of each other. We need corrected vision. This is *"A Course in* Miracles*"* central focus. We will collectively develop an intuitive understanding of each other as living spiritual beings, not just as human beings limited to physical bodies. *"ACIM"* uses the term Self also as a symbol of our higher spiritual identity. This is the central archetypal energy now descending into our conscious awareness, both as individuals and in the collective mind. This archetype presents itself in our consciousness as images and motifs, known by the results they produce. Our spiritual goal is to realize the content of this central archetype, the Christ or Self, as our living reality. This is the mighty sea to which all rivers run.

As more of us commit to this "inner work" of awakening to the Self, the process begins to quicken. As we commence a course of action, the time it takes to initiate Self-awakening will shorten. What at one time was uncommon knowledge, intimating from the collective unconscious, now sweeps into the individual conscious awareness of many. The critical mass of those required to initiate this quickening is not known. Like many of the mysteries of our Apocalyptic Myth, we can only suggest a number. But, in time, we will amass a nucleus forming the "critical few" necessary to begin our acceleration. This quickening or acceleration is the "Celestial Speed-Up."

When more join in a movement to awaken the greater Self, terror emboldened by the "Archetype of the Apocalypse" will lose it grip on individuals and cultures, particularity those fixated on the "End Times" phenomenon. Armageddon need not be; we will find release from our fear of the Apocalypse. It waits behind a thin veil of disbelief. It will lift in a holy instant. And in that instant we will see how lovely the face of Christ appears, even on those we call our attackers.

Jung used the term "individuation" to describe the process of Self-realization because he wanted to avoid prejudice from Christian and non-Christian religions. Relating the concept of awakening to the

Christ with the concept of Self-realization is not necessarily found in psychological theories. I do so because *"ACIM"* is focused toward Western religions, but the process has different names in every tradition. Its outcome is the "universal experience" which is necessary for our survival from horrors of the Apocalypse. It can and will overcome our conscious and unconscious fears of "End Times."

Let me repeat: a universal experience is not only possible, but necessary. I believe the Celestial Speed-Up is that universal experience. It is the central focus of awakening to our greatest potential as individuals and as entire cultures. It will rise above language and religious differences so that all can hear and experience its message. It has many names until we can all recognize the one. It patiently waits behind a thin veil of denial.

In our Western cultures, we alternate between literal and inerrant religious beliefs on one extreme, then swing to symbolic and metaphorical perspectives on the other. Cyclical patterns can be traced through the centuries. Our recent rash of literalism began in the late 19th Century. It is in full cycle again. When ensnared in a belief of religious inerrancy, we tend to attack each other like trapped rats. Instigated by fear, it appears as "Holy Crusades" and "Wars on Terror." We are unconscious players in a great passion of hopeless travail.

The War on Terror

We suffer yet another world war. The Children of Abraham - Jews, Christians and Muslims - are fighting evil on the faces of each other. Defending holy ground, we each await the appearance of a prophet or messiah. Peace is of no consequence, destruction of each other is justified. Cultures now clash on a mission to destroy the antichrist. Looking within the midst of each other, we cannot agree on its identity - yet it preoccupies each group. We must answer Jung's question again: will we survive our global war on terror in our outer world, while a solution patiently waits in our unconscious minds?

Our answer to the question to Jung is the same. Yes, we will survive if enough of us do our inner work. Answering this call to forgiveness is our inner work. The process begins by learning to see those we call evil as our saviors. It does not require action, but just a "little willingness" to change our mind. The purpose of this work is to introduce a process that initiates our awakening to the "universal experience" referenced in opening quotations from *"The Clarification of Terms"* following the *"Manual for Teachers,"* accompanying *"A Course in Miracles."* This experience of awakening, in most cases, will be preceded by a period of discomfort and confusion we call our personal apocalypse: a time of self doubt and discord. But this is a transitory phase which precedes our personal awakening. It is followed by the appearance of our greater spiritual identity, now coming into our conscious awareness. This is the Second Coming as foretold in the Apocalyptic Myth. This is the Christ returning to our awakened mind. An accelerated appearance of this awareness in many is the purpose of this Celestial Speed-Up. As others undertake their personal role in this "Speed-Up," the process will initiate, then quicken and accelerate.

The next seven Chapters gives a more detailed description on how the Celestial Speed-Up will be initiated. We will redefine certain terms and concepts from the Book of Revelation, based on *"A Course in Miracles."* The final chapter gives recommendations for those who wish to undertake the process for change and awakening. It suggests a method of small group study as a solution. When two or more come together for a spiritual purpose, our fear of the Apocalypse has no power. But we each have a process for our own individual awakening, hence individuation.

The unpublished manuscript given by the scribes to the Edgar Cayce Library (the Association for Research and Enlightenment or A.R.E.) became known as the *Hugh Lynn Cayce* manuscript of *"ACIM,"* named after Cayce's son. It is now available for personal study along with other editions of the original manuscripts.* Any of these may scrve as a text for small group "reading" and discussion and as a starter text for those who wish to take their place in our call to awaken the Christ-Self. This is the invitation issued by The Book of Revelation, when viewed from the perspective of *"A Course in Miracles."* According

---

* *The first edition of this work included the first four chapters of the Hugh Lynn Cayce (HLC) edition of "ACIM." At that time, few copies of this version were available. Since then, many copies of the original manuscript (the Urtext) from which the HLC version was derived are now available. The first edition was published in 1975. You can get copies online in PDF or at most bookstores. Accordingly, the HLC chapters have been deleted from the second edition*

to its Author, our individual Course of awakening is inevitable. Only the time we choose to take it is optional.

May you be blessed with God's speed as you take your place among the "critical few" necessary to initiate this Celestial Speed-Up.

Chapter 1

The Celestial Speed-Up,

The Universal Awakening

"What you look forward to has already come,

but you do not recognize it."

(Jesus the Christ - The Gospel of Thomas, Verse 51)

Beginning the Inner Work, the Universal Experience

"A Course in Miracles" (ACIM) is a 600 plus page text accompanied by a *"Workbook"* with 365 daily lessons. Among other things it includes a *"Manuel for Teachers"* for those wishing to take its message beyond intellectual pursuits. More than 1.5 million copies have been sold in many languages. Its implications are entering mainstream Christianity in the United States. The entire text was channeled and the author's identity is still being debated. We do know it was scribed by two teaching doctor's of psychology at Columbia University's College of Physicians and Surgeons, but they were not its author. They were only the ones chosen to record and edit the message. Their text and literary edits contain a powerful message about the Book of Revelation.

When "End Times" terms and symbols are redefined, their age-old riddles are resolved. Restored is a sense of mystery and awe, both of which are appropriate for the Apocalyptic Myth. This former tale of woe is no longer set in stone as literal and inerrant prophecy. When viewed from this new perspective, it initiates the process of awakening our Christ-Self. It is already a part of our collective and unconscious mind. As more begin to study the process, the rate of "unlearning" our inerrant myth will increase. Being able to see old concepts from this new perspective is the end result of reconsidering our ancient misperceptions. As "unlearning" accelerates in a rapid manner, the

"Celestial Speed-Up" will occur. We have experienced "speed-ups" before; they will be detailed in the following chapters.

Like forgiveness, "unlearning" has a unique meaning in *"ACIM."* It is the process of reconsidering inerrant decisions made long ago. These unconscious, yet literal, decisions are chiseled in granite. Becoming willing to see our choices differently is the only requirement to initiate the "unlearning" process. We each have an internal teacher that will make the corrected choice for us when we are ready and ask. As these new choices enter the conscious mind, they will become collective. Uncommon knowledge now becomes a common understanding. This is the universal experience which is necessary. This is the real meaning of the Second Coming.

Pre-Christian Jews sought a messiah to lead battle against Roman captors. For Christians and later Muslims, God did not send a military leader to make war. Instead, He sent a savior and prophet to teach lessons of love and forgiveness. Two thousand years later, we repeat our search for a military leader to march forces of good against evil in a Battle at Armageddon. Fortunately, this savior and prophet has already returned, offering love and forgiveness. This message is the thought system now in our minds. It is waiting on our "little willingness" to give its blessing of freedom from fear of the apocalypse. This Messiah and his message will show us correction. The concepts for both now reside in a "higher place of learning" in our unconscious mind. It is coming into our conscious awareness, never to leave again.

Seeing With the Spiritual Eye

The process of awakening and its implications, as contained by symbols in the Book of Revelation, will be outlined in this work. When properly discerned, they will awaken us to realities of a new freedom offered by our internal teacher. Fear's grip is strong. We cannot withdraw our fixation on horrendous aspects of the myth's tales. This message of forgiveness is faint in our minds. Loosening our choke hold of fear, we see beyond obstacles; and can hear its message. But, we need help from an internal teacher, one who is personal to each of us.

The author of *"A Course in Miracles"* used the name "Spiritual Eye" to describe a direct communication link between each individual person and a universal deity Christians call God. This author, who describes himself as an "Elder Brother," gives new meaning to the Apocalyptic Myth. He explains that the purpose of the Book of Revelation is to introduce a process awakening our Divine or Christ-Self within. As this knowledge descends into our conscious awareness, prophecies begin to be fulfilled. We need not fear these outcomes; they are not forecasts of doom. As more awaken to these new realities, their effects become intuitive, then collective.

It is the function of our Elder Brother, in conjunction with the Spiritual Eye's communication link, to plan and execute our awakening. The Spiritual Eye is a name used in the Hugh Lynn Cayce Edition of "ACIM." It has many names. Jungians would equate this to an "ego-Self axis." It remains unconscious until it emerges in the Self-realization process, where it brings a conscious connection of our smaller ego-self to a Greater Reality.

This process of "coming again" is not limited to Western religious teachings. Many non-Christian religions use a similar concept. Integrating the many names into one brings an attitude of forgiveness and understanding. Seeing our interest the same as others accelerates our arrival at this point. The process of awakening to a higher or Christ-Self is an individual universal experience; no one holds a patent. To comprehend its nature, we need an encounter with this knowledge. This is the universal experience which is not only possible, but necessary. We must escape the ego's hold of fear that retards our approach to our Christ-Self's awareness; it is already in our mind.

We can only attempt to define the experience of awakening. This is like the East Indian tale of 10 blind men describing an elephant, each holding a different appendage. Using their means of touch and smell, they imagined the whole of the elephant based on individual perceptions. While each was accurate in their description, not one could describe the whole elephant. We, too, are grasping to share our own perspective. This is knowledge of the Christ or Self; it is seeking us as well. Buddha offered an observation, "If any one of us knew the truth, we would have all told our brothers by now." We can call on those who have experienced greater levels of understanding to assist us in laying a sure-footed way. Such a Pathfinder is in our mind now, awaiting recognition. *A Course in Miracles* is only one such pathway.

Freud, Jung and the Individuated Ego

A religious or spiritual experience illuminates a means for each of us to find our true spiritual nature. Jung's process of individuation is another path. Many believe Jung experienced the highest levels of individuation as he and Freud rediscovered and studied the unconscious. The author of "ACIM" suggests Freud really did understand the unconscious mind correctly. Unfortunately, he failed to call upon a Divine Guide that was given him to initiate the process of unlearning our ego's grip of fear. His experience of peace was elusive. Even with his intellectual knowledge, Freud never learned to listen to the Spirit within.

Unlearning is a key concept in "ACIM." It is directed at removing blocks preventing our experience of peace of mind. This assumption understands we are fully capable of receiving Divine love in our own lives. We need do nothing more to accept this gift of forgiveness than be willing to remove obstacles. Unlearning is the process of removing these obstacles in both the conscious and unconscious mind. This was Freud's dilemma; he needed the help of a learned Teacher, which he had, but never used. Jung had a different experience.

We must explore the integrated relationship of individuation and religion and, specifically how they relate to the Book of Revelation. Jung and Freud were the first to popularize these concepts in a secular format for Western minds. Their source materials were many. They included: mythology, Eastern religions, alchemy, Christian texts and parapsychology. Each describes a pathway for awakening to our higher Self. It took their enlightened minds to see beyond the symbols and realize the similarity of processes. From this perspective, the symbols in The Book of Revelation redefine the Apocalyptic Myth. It becomes a guidebook to awakening our Divinity, the Christ-Self, residing in our unconscious mind.

According to Stephen Hoeller in the *Gnostic Jung,* the concepts of individuation were affirmed by Jung from other great spiritual teachers. One of Jung's descriptions is taken from St. Ignatius of Loyola, founder of the Jesuit Order. In four stages, he suggests we must: (1) become aware of our descent from unity with a higher source; (2) pay "due and careful" respect to the source; (3) be intelligent and responsible with what it compels us to accomplish; and (4) see the "optimum degree" of knowledge for developing our life

16

and becoming whole. This is our understanding of the Christ-Self within our psyche, the totality of our being. As it awakens and becomes a living experience, it flows into conscious awareness, redirecting ourselves and touching the lives of others.

The Inner Journey

The inner journey required to initiate this process is not always voluntary – or even obvious – to the participant. Ascetics who commit to a life of meditation and prayer are aware of their calling. They are in touch with the process and have wise guidance before undertaking this journey. For those attempting to continue a sectarian life, commands from the Self can be disruptive to our material goals. We are not always ready to acknowledge this purpose. In mid-life, Jung was so overwhelmed with the affects of individuation he retired to build a tower of stone with mortar and trowel. His process of self-awakening became disorienting and he felt "suspended in mid-air." He had not found his footings in teaching or practicing medicine. For those in this grip, the individuation process swings like a pendulum, with great accomplishments and unbelievable lows – and stops at every station in between. When inflated with triumphs, life holds few miseries. Deflated with failure, its burdens bring despair and a dim view of the horizon.

Our inflated egos are the child who leads the marching band, but doesn't know the steps. This smaller self, our ego, expands far beyond knowledge of St. Ignatius of Loyola's attitude of "due and careful" respect for the greater Self. We must learn the march before we lead the band. These steps are the life experiences we choose. They direct us through never-ending cycles, presenting lessons over and again. We celebrate great victories and endure hopeless defeats. At times, they appear to carry no meaning. This is the process of individuation, winding its path through our lives for an optimal learning experience. It is fraught with peril; sometimes, it takes its toll. For those who endure, a breakthrough occurs. Into our dismal lives appears a light of hope. A faint glimmer of knowledge expands into our conscious awareness. Eventually, it becomes a beacon with which we see purpose and meaning beyond our polarities of triumph and despair. This breakthrough, or ray of light, is our communication link to the higher Self. The Cayce version of *"A Course in Miracles"* calls this link the Spiritual Eye.

This is only one aspect of individuation. It brings about an awareness of our greater Self, the center of our being waiting in our unconscious mind. Our smaller self – the child leading the band – falsely imitates the character of an experienced director, until he leads the troupe down a dead-end street. So do we attempt to play God. It is the higher Self that orders and structures our life, whether we are conscious of its choices or not. The inflated ego gets pricked at many stages in our experiences; it deflates in a whirlwind, withering to a new low. We are now Job on a dung heap, scraping our boils with chards of glass. These cycles of inflation and deflation continue until we can hear the voice of our communication link from the Spirit within. These endless swings between opposite poles will dampen. Eventually, some level of meaning and purpose appears with a new vision for the future. The apocalypse of our ego nears its end. We will survive this personal Armageddon.

This is the cycle of struggle we endure to acquire an attitude of "due and careful" respect. It was Jung's experience of this endless cycle of inflation and deflation that he described as our pathway to experiencing the higher Self. Trial and error opens channels to communicate. We learn to listen with an attentive ear. This process of awakening involves right sizing the ego. These are the dark nights of the Soul. They are the desert experiences of Elijah, Moses and Jesus of Nazareth. Each was banished to the sands before they ascended the mountain top. When trained to listen, the individuated or enlightened ego knows how to be right sized. It learns to listen for knowledge of our greater good. The process for every person is different, hence the name individuation. For those who survive mentally intact, the end result is an awakening to our higher Self, the Christ within. This personal rebirth takes its own form in each religion.

Lao Tzu and Following the Light

Knowledge of this process predates our Western culture. It can be found in many Eastern religions. There is a passage in the I Ching which describes the individuated person as one who has spiritual powers which emanate from deep within. The "*I Ching,*" some believe, was written in the sixth century B.C. by sage Lao Tzu. It describes these enlighten individuals as ones who can influence and support others without either party being aware of how this happens. Some are able to comprehend the mysteries and workings of the universe through contemplation of these divine laws. They become aware of its effects on themselves and others. No longer are they unconscious actors on a stage, wearing a mask and playing an assigned role. They become director and observer, properly positioned for optimum learning and teaching. The production is now perceived as the whole. Their persona is only an outer mask; it covers the true Self.

The enlightened director knows which part to play, which parts to assign, when to speak and when to be silent. Working for a greater good, these individuals may not be seen as the director at all. But they "understand," or in the original meaning, "stand under." The smaller ego, or little self, now serves the greater Self. It "stands under" with virtue and strength. This is the way as proscribed by Lao Tzu. Here is a translation of Verse Twenty-Seven from the *Tao Te Ching*."

Tao Te Ching

A good walker leaves no tracks;
A good speaker makes no slips;
A good reckoner needs no tally.
A good door needs no lock.
Yet no one can open it.
Good bindings need no knots:
Yet no one can loosen it.

Therefore the sage takes care of all men
And abandons no one.
He takes care of all things
And abandons nothing.
This is called "following the light."

What is a good man?
The teacher of a bad man?
What is a bad man?
A good man's charge.
If the teacher is not respected,
And the student not cared for,
Confusion will arise, however clever one is.
This is the crux of the mystery.

Self-Actualization and Maslow's Hierarchy of Needs

Abrams Maslow developed a means of explaining human behavior based on motivation. His theories suggested a reality that we each are motivated to obtain our highest state of development. He called this "self-actualization." There are many similarities with Jung's process of individuation. They cannot be equated, but like the blind men with the elephant, each appears to be describing some part of a process leading to a greater whole.

Maslow's research detailed specific behaviors and characteristics of individuals who are self-actualized: they are realistically oriented and able to accept other people for whom they are. Spontaneous in their thinking, these self-actualized individuals are emotionally and behaviorally mature. They respond with a problem centered, rather than ego-centered, approach. They have a need for privacy. Being autonomous, they are independent thinkers who remain true to themselves in the face of rejection. Their fresh approach to life is accompanied by "mystic or oceanic" experiences which some could describe as a religious or spiritual breakthrough. Having developed a deep connection to life, self-actualized individuals identify with the suffering and pain of all mankind. Their internal structure is democratic; they judge others as individuals from a highly developed ethical value system that may not conform to their culture. Movement through the following stages begins at the bottom and transcends upward. A diagram offers characteristics of these progressions.

Maslow's Hierarchy of Needs

Self-Actualization: *morality, creativity, spontaneity, problem solving, lack of prejudice, acceptance of facts.*

Self-Esteem: *confidence, achievement, respects for others, respect   for self.*

Love/ Belonging: *friendship, family, sexual intimacy.*

Safety: *security of body, of employment, of resources, of morality.*

Physiological: *breathing, food, water, sex, sleep, homeostasis, excretion.*

Maslow believed there are those among us who transcend our sense of "being only a person in a body." These individuals no longer see themselves as a smaller self (or ego-self), but part of a grander scheme. He called these insights "peak experiences." They provide a path to achieve personal growth, integration and fulfillment. These "peak experiences" are a unifying, ego-transcending awareness. They open doors to our unconscious that heretofore have been closed. Through these doors, individuals having transcending experiences find a sense of purpose which integrates daily life with personal growth.

Those most likely to have peak experiences are self-actualized, mature, healthy and self-fulfilled. According to Maslow, all individuals are capable of these experiences. Those who do not have "peak experiences" may be depressed or even denying the events. It was his belief we have an innate urge to self-actualize and will even transcend the sense of the smaller or ego-self, the part believing it is trapped in a body. Such an experience points toward an encounter with the greater Self. This is what Jung described as a "breakthrough" into conscious awareness; it is experiential.

While these processes function at all ages, the need to individuate or experience self-actualization becomes acute at midlife for adults. For many, this is a time when life's meaning and purpose comes forward to claim their day of reckoning. The death of parents or close loved ones, failed careers, illnesses, vicissitudes of parenting and even great successes become our albatrosses. Seeking the ends of our travail does not necessarily bring understanding, only the ends. Beginning to see our life-changing experiences as a never-ending cycle of inflation and deflation is a beginning.

Dark shadows from our unconscious mind present themselves anonymously. Limitations long avoided now sit on our doorstep. For those who seek some form of understanding, what arrives is a glimpse of our transcendent identity. Here order runs to greets confusion. Receiving some map of a grander scheme becomes gratifying in and of itself. Loosening our grip of identification as this smaller ego-self, the one trapped in a body, is a start. This is the rich young man who was told to "sell all he had" and follow the Christ. This calling cannot be avoided, only delayed. Our day of judgment has come, at last.

Individuation and Jesus of Nazareth, the Christ

One aspect of individuation is the need for conscious expression of our long-repressed and spiritual needs. These will emerge from the unconscious, whether invited or not. While most call it a "crisis experience," it is actually a warning to take full advantage of our desires and capabilities now hidden in the unconscious. These are life's aims begging for expression. Right sizing our egos is the first step of integration. The process of individuating has no timeframe. It consists of a series of metamorphoses (the death-rebirth cycle), such as birth, infancy, puberty, adulthood and midlife. If one can acknowledge the individuation process, the ego or smaller self no longer holds center stage for our conscious universe. In addition to right sizing the ego, Maslow suggested we must make some sort of peace with our mortality. This is an unavoidable understanding; the body we inhabit will not last forever. We no longer fear death as our personal apocalypse on the horizon.

For the midlife crisis, Jung suggests a turning of life may have its cure. One prescription is returning to a dedicated spiritual practice. However, many are disinclined to take up the trappings of traditional religions. For these individuals, Jung suggested his own approach to therapy and analysis. Edward Edinger was considered the dean of Jungian psychology here in the United States. He studied with Jung in Zurich and published many titles on the subjects of psychology and religion. Two of his publications, *"Ego and Archetype"* and *"Archetype of the Apocalypse,"* are referred to frequently in this work.

Edinger suggested Jesus of Nazareth was one who struggled in rising above his identity as a human body, accepting his invitation to individuate. Some sources suggest that Jesus had been prepared for his ascension by the priestly orders into which he was born. Many believe he was a member of the Essenes of Qumran, home of the Dead Sea Scrolls. It was during his baptism that Jesus was visited by the Holy Spirit. He was submerged by a learned teacher, John the Baptist, perhaps also an Essene.

The First Coming into Collective Awareness

When Jesus of Nazareth emerged from baptism, he became the "anointed one" imbued with the Spirit. If this can be equated to the awakened or individuated ego, he could now draw understanding from a "higher place of learning" in the unconscious mind. He was fully aware of his role as the Enlightened One, Christ and Teacher. In myths and dreams, water can be a symbol for our unconscious mind, or that dark place we must enter to find a light of truth. When Jesus was baptized, he was introduced to this journey by someone who knew this path: John the Baptist. The metamorphosis complete, he could now walk on water and was no longer at the behest of the unconscious mind. He was functioning above an endless pendulum swinging between inflation and deflation. He was free to live at the direction of the Christ-Self. He had found his way. We could think of this as a "peak or oceanic experience" that was collective in nature. It was so powerful it began the awakening of our entire Western way of thinking. It loosened the collective ego's hold on our belief of being bodies alone. This was the First Coming of the "Anointed One" into our Western conscious mind; we now await a Second Coming.

Jesus' birth was an expression of the Immaculate Conception in the minds of Mary and Joseph. They accepted their part in bringing the concept of Christ as the only begotten Son of God into our conscious mind. This is the whole and complete "Son of God" or "Son of Man" in each individual person. In our Western mindset, many have assigned this identity exclusively to the Nazarene. But can this level of spiritual understanding be contained in the mind of one man, or must it be the possession of all mankind? We still seek collective recognition of a Universal Divinity.

As a culture, our knowledge or experiential awareness of this greater identity has been forgotten. "*ACIM*" would say we have chosen not to remember. We forgot our spiritual identity and where we came from. The Book of Revelation foretells of knowledge at this level of understanding. It gives us steps to attain this greater awakening and tells us how to bring it into broad public consciousness. This is the Rapture. We will be lifted up, into our unconscious minds, to a new experience of the Christ-Self. "*ACIM*" would say we will rise to a complete understanding of the mind that was also in Christ Jesus. As more of us have this "peak experience," it will descend, entering into our broad conscious awareness at an increasing rate. This accelerated awareness into our conscious mind is the "Celestial Speed-Up." Christ will have come again.

The Second Coming and the Celestial Speed-Up

Attaining this collective awareness is the real meaning of the Second Coming. This knowledge was in the mind of Jesus of Nazareth, the Awakened Christ. It is now coming into a greater conscious acceptance for all of us. This is experiential knowledge, not intellectual. When a sufficient number of students undertake this awakening process, it will initiate a quickening in the unlearning process called the "Celestial Speed-Up" by the author of *"ACIM."* This phrase was omitted from the published editions of *"ACIM."* The "Speed-Up" has a significant role for each of us when we choose to accept our position as a teacher of God. All of us are being called to accept this commission. In Christian terms, this is God's Plan of Salvation. Many have answered this call to re-awaken our higher spiritual Self. The real purpose of the Book of Revelation is to guide each of us as we unlock the symbolism of terms and concepts hidden within its allegories.

As you read forward, you will learn more about the two doctors of psychology at Columbia University's College of Physicians and Surgeons who scribed *"ACIM."* These were professionals who were published and well respected in their fields of research. They developed teaching methods for medical doctors at a leading school. They were selected by the author of *"ACIM"* to scribe the text, then edit and publish the work for the purpose of reintroducing a spiritual teaching which needed a new understanding. As medical professionals, both felt their preparation for this task had begun in previous lives, long before they became teaching psychologists. Each recounted personal premonitions and experiences in several publications which predated their assignment. This was their processes of individuation or self-actualization, preparing them for a divine purpose. They implied it happened over many lifetimes.

We each are called to this process of unlearning life's goals we assumed at a young age. These aims are of great import, based on what we have learned from family and society. It is difficult to redirect priorities. However, we must unlearn these assumptions to accept our new role in the Plan of Salvation. This is the program for awakening the Christ-Self in every man, woman and child. Unlearning is the process of reconsidering the importance placed on self-image, goals and perceptions about others and ourselves. To do this, we need the help of a spiritual guide with a vision of a new destination. We want someone who knows where He is going. A bridge to Heaven lies before us.

Celestial is another name for Heaven, the ultimate dwelling place of our greater Self, the Christ-Self. This is the transcendent part of the unconscious mind that has never left the presence of God. Our awakening to and awareness of this identity is the purpose of *"ACIM."* It advises us the Christ-Self will retain its many names and pathways until we can understand them all as one. *"ACIM"* has been written in Christian terms to be understood by Western minds. It is a focused teaching and will not speak to everyone.

The Speed-Up is "a quickening" or acceleration in our unlearning. Visually, you may see this as an avalanche gaining momentum as it descends. The mass assumes proportions at some point in time, so great that it takes on a life of its own. In this application, experience of the Christ-Self will become autonomous. It will appear in the various names and forms as necessary so that each individual will understand this presence without question or hesitation. This is fulfillment of the Celestial Speed-Up. It is an accelerated awakening to our Divine or Christ-Self that resides in Heaven and in our unconscious mind. It awaits our conscious recognition to descend into experiential awareness.

The two doctors at Columbia University asked the author of *"ACIM"* why they were chosen to participate in this Celestial Speed-Up. He explained that everyone has a part in accelerating the process of individualized learning (or unlearning) to awaken our collective Divinity and actualize the Christ-Self. Their part was scribing *"ACIM."*

Each of us has a role in this Plan to salvage the future from our obsession with self-destruction. The author of *"ACIM"* has the responsibility of making those assignments. When we are ready and ask, our part in the Plan will be given. This is the purpose of the individualized learning process.

Unlearning the Apocalyptic Myths of End Times

An important part in this awakening process is reconsidering our understanding of the Book of Revelation. We must rethink its myths of the Apocalypse, Armageddon and The End of Time. The *"ACIM"* author has given new definitions for such terms such as Revelation, Rapture, Second Coming, Tribulation and antichrist. These new meanings speak of a process for personally awakening the Christ-Self within. We must unlearn our misunderstandings that have evolved from centuries of fear and ignorance. The process is clear and straight forward. Offer just a "little willingness" to experience this reawakening and, in time, the Second Coming of Christ into our conscious awareness is assured.

Our misunderstandings about the Apocalyptic Myth have created a fictional account of and "end" to this world; it keeps us entombed in fear. This unreality is our ego's horror of awakening to the Christ-Self. We project this outward onto the unsuspecting: friends, neighbors, loved ones and enemies. This happens with individuals as well as collectively in cultures. It protects us from the ones we call evil. In fact, these "evil ones" are our best teachers. Our protagonist becomes an instructor. According to Lao Tzu, the good man needs the bad man (or protagonist) as a student to function. This is our charge: to see innocence in the ones we call evil. We need a mirror to reflect the Christ-Self within. Metaphorically, it can only be seen in this manner. My enemy now appears as my Savior; we greet the Christ in each other.

Words are but symbols of symbols, so the images seen on these pages are there to awaken a truth already in our minds. No one can intervene in this process save our Spiritual Teacher, the Elder Brother. He and the Spiritual Eye are the internal entities who will guide each of us on a pathway to our self-actualization, or the individuation of the Christ-Self. This is the experience that is necessary before we can collectively move beyond theology. This is the "Love of God" experienced on earth. This is the force propelling the "Celestial Speed-Up."

Cultures on a Collision Course

Each of us needs to consider the critical juncture at which we stand, not only as a culture but our entire human thought system. It is imperative we rethink our Myth of the Apocalypse if we are to survive a real Armageddon. What has evolved into our conscious minds is nothing more than justification for death and destruction. This Myth and its legends are gross misunderstandings. It manifests itself in continual destruction of communities, families and individuals. This is justified in the name of preparing for a Messiah to return. Meanwhile, we seek to find and destroy the real antichrist. This is not prophecy; this is insanity. A Messiah is coming! But it is descending into our conscious awareness, not just as a physical body or as a leader taking us into battle.

It is incumbent upon each of us to look at what has evolved in Judeo-Christian and Islamic religions. Essentially, both descended from the children of Abraham. We have developed tales of woe with the hatred and intensity of a sibling rivalry. Each faction includes an Apocalyptic Myth of End Times, including a Judgment Day. Each version prescribes mass murder and abominations known as Armageddon. All foretell of an antichrist who will lead battles of their respective forces against the other. Each sees the other as the evil ones. Even if we don't swear allegiance to the Myth, it is collective and in our unconscious minds. It now prompts action and inactions that support a scenario of world destruction. The dark shadows of our Christian culture, which we have hidden deep in our unconscious, are immediate and visible to the Islamic culture. And what the Islamic religion has hidden, deep inside themselves is visible to us and becomes our justification for attacks. We are cultures on an unconscious collision course, powered by a collective transpersonal energy, with forces greater than a natural catastrophe. We must become willing to see this differently.

As a society, we must reconsider this tale of death and destruction. If we don't, it will come to fruition. Not everyone needs do this to halt the process; we only need a critical few. Ten righteous men can raise a city. If enough of us do our inner work, as Jung suggested, the awakening will be initiated. We are the critical few. Our task is at hand. A solution has been provided.

The Unlearning Process in Group Study

I encourage you to obtain a copy of "*ACIM*" text for a study group. It was a belief of the "*ACIM*" scribes that unlearning can be accomplished in small-group study. A small group comprises fewer than 20-25 students in one setting. Since it is important to place each group participant on equal footing, it is preferable groups remain small in number. Reading, discussion and questioning are critical to the unlearning process. I call these groups "Circles of Forgiveness." While group study is not for everyone, it is the suggested means by this work, and essential for those undertaking the process of unlearning. Chapter 7 will offer methods, tools and suggestions on how to start an unlearning group. An internal Teacher will show the way to learn forgiveness in a circle.

The terms Spiritual Eye and "Celestial Speed-Up" have not been edited or removed from the ACIM text (the Hugh Lynn Cayce Edition). The author uses a symphonic means of writing. Critical messages are reintroduced over and again in different contexts with new applications. These awaken certain questions in our minds. They need to be verbalized and then discussed to clarify the intent and prepare for an answer. The questions are almost always answered in the next few paragraphs. This core message is set forth in each chapter. All the tools needed are available when we decide to accept our part in this "Speed-Up." The group-study process will accelerate the unlearning process. When two or more come together for this holy purpose, miraculous things will happen. Studying together truly becomes a course inspiring miracles!

As more decide to study "ACIM" in small groups, the process of unlearning will become ingrained. Questioning misunderstandings will become predictable. All that is required is enough self-restraint to allow open discussion. Questions should be refined as they arise within the group. They are being brought forward for a purpose. Allow these questions to be defined, and then muster the patience to proceed on to the next paragraph. There, you will find the answers. As study groups normalize, the timing for each of these revelations will become apparent. You will know when to read, when to discuss and when to go on to the next paragraph. The process' main focus is to prompt questions already in our mind, refine the questions and then allow answers to be given by the internal Teacher. The answer is always in the next few paragraphs. Symbols will be defined in your mind as you are gently ushered through this reawakening process by your internal Teacher.

The process is simple. The difficulty is using restraint while learning to listen to the internal Teacher. This is the "ACIM" author using his ingenuity by allowing each group to define and answer questions individualized for their "Circle of Forgiveness." After a group forms, it develops its own patterns of study and reading. It is amazing how, given patience, a personalized unlearning process progresses in time for everyone.

Awakening the Internal Teacher

Remember, we don't need an external teacher; we need to awaken our "internal" Teacher. Keep this ever in the forefront of your mind. Group facilitators are responsible for sensing the pace of reading, questioning and discussion prior to moving on. The ability to follow the questions that arise in our minds is the process of awakening the voice of our internal Teacher. It may speak as a fellow student across the room sharing personal experiences to resolve his own dilemmas. Our internal Teacher has a unique way of matching questioning minds with common solutions. Facilitators are the matchmakers in this most holy process. A calm reassurance will validate answers as you read the next paragraph. It is a simple process.

"ACIM" will present common misunderstandings from the Book of Revelation. When taken as literal prophecy, they create fear and trepidation and become sources of tremendous world conflicts. As groups begin reading "ACIM," a cleansing effect will be experienced. In order for a collective effort to initiate, enough of us must undertake this task. Our egos are terrorized by the thought of our Christ-Self coming into conscious awareness. The threat is an apocalyptic nightmare that preoccupies our mind with horrific predictions of death and destruction. These precede the appearance of our greater Self coming into broad conscious realization: "... and their torture will not stop, day or night, forever and ever."* This threat is followed in the in the Book of Revelation's Epilogue by a wonderful promise: "Then let all who are thirsty come: all who want it shall have the water of life and have it free" (Revelation 20:10).

This is the crux of the mystery, the ebb and flow of our paradox. What follows on the next page are excerpts from "ACIM, Manual for Teachers" in the chapter entitled, How Will the World End? The answer has nothing to do with a horrific end to our world. It only requires us to reconsider the apocalyptic concepts that haunt our minds. Our egos will resist this change at all cost. Do not be discouraged; read on and begin the inner work. Our day of awakening is near.

Here is a description of how the world will end from "The Manuel for Teachers" accompanying *"A Course in Miracles."* I have placed it in stanzas to emphasize the poetic nature of the prophecy.

How Will the World End?

The world will end in joy,

Because it is a place of sorrow.

The world will end in peace,

Because it is a place of war.

The world will end in laughter,

Because it is a place of tears.

One sin perfectly forgiven,

By one Teacher of God,

Makes Salvation complete.

Yet this we cannot understand;

Our final lesson where unity is restored.

Until forgiveness is complete,

This world has a purpose.

For here is born a gentle Savior,

Wherein sin was made and guilt seemed real.

He brings the ending of the world,

When all things have been judged rightly.

This seems to be a long, long while away.

But time stands still, waiting on this goal.

One holy instant can bring Atonement.

For it is just as easy to forgive one sin,

As to forgive them all.

To turn hell into Heaven,

Is the function of God's Teachers.

Only trust and be willing,

For no lesson is too great to be learned,

No sin to heinous to be forgiven.

There is a final lesson,

Which brings ending of the world.

Yet it cannot be grasped,

By those not prepared to leave,

And go beyond this world's tiny reaches.

Offer only a "little willingness,"

To escape this hold and enjoin trust.

The world will end with the

Benediction of holiness upon it.

And when not one thought of sin remains,

This world is over.

(Source material: *Manuel for Teachers, A Course in Miracles*.)

Chapter 2

Grip of the Apocalypse

Western Christianity is in a state of despair.

It has lost the mysteries of its religion.

Without mystery there is no spirit,

Without spirit there is no love.

Without love, no message,

In love's void; chaos resides.

Blessed be the name of the Lord.

Why We Choose Destruction

A part of the "unlearning" process is to review common beliefs about Apocalyptic Myth in our conscious and unconscious minds. We as a religious culture are firmly in the grip of a fearful tale that has no clear ending. To some, it is an obsession which requires prophetic explanation. We must ask the question: Why are we obsessed with a fear of "End Times?" Our answers will reveal these hidden horrors in our unconscious mind. These are identifiable by non-Western cultures, yet not by us. They have been blotted from our awareness. They fuel our endless conflicts. We must look at the log in our own eye, before pointing to a speck in our brother's. These are cultural beliefs we hold dear to our hearts, pledging never to release. We have taken a solemn vow: we will never look at these hidden fears and horrors we entreat with our egos.

So pervasive is our fanaticism over "End Times," economic engines and social structures propelling our way of life dismantle before our eyes. There should be outrage! We are like horses running into fire. Fears supporting myths of Armageddon lay unconscious, covered by blinders. Operating under a banner of apocalyptic terror, we waste human resources fighting an image of evil veiled on foreign faces. No one can bear to count the bodies of innocent men, women and children killed in these wars of conquest. So great is our grief we cannot look, even to weep, upon the flag-draped coffins of our own children. These sights release wretched pain, reflecting the carnage of our "End Times" nightmares. Are these "holy" missions a fulfillment of apocalyptic prophecies? Soldiers with a gun in one hand and a Bible in the other appear conflicted.

While starving for spiritual renewal, our focus remains on inerrant prophecies sustained by religious morality; we forego spiritual healing. A cup empty of forgiveness cannot nourish its flock. Those who thirst for the essence of God must take communion from a different chalice. We need to see things differently.

Our malady suffers cultural symptoms. Metaphorically, we consume alcoholic spirits or even drugs to quench this craving for spiritual revival. Our eternal flame of Light becomes extinguished while we addict our children to tobacco. Snuffed with fear, we fail at attempts to rekindle our precious flame of spiritual renewal. Desire for spiritual intimacy with the Christ Child goes unfilled. We molest children instead. These are "signs of the times." A solitary focus on morality cannot awaken the spirit within, nor can moral legislation salvage the faithful. We grasp desperately for repentance with the anguish of a sinner in death's throes. Legalistic beliefs only smother our spirit of rebirth. These metaphors signal our fear of "End Times."

But there is another way.

The Book of Revelation is not a prescription for death and destruction. It is a pathway to answering a call for spiritual renewal offered to every man, woman and child. We have shrouded our greater spiritual good behind a thin veil. Rather than look at our fear within, we project it out. This projection becomes a seven-headed monster that will lead the forces of evil against good. In reality, this leviathan is our resistance to accepting forgiveness from within. This monster is our "Myth of the Apocalypse" that shrouds our reprieve.

Doomsday Scenarios

The apocalyptic *"Left Behind"* series has sold more than 60 million copies of a fictionalized account from the Book of Revelation. It offers a doomsday view of "End Times." For many, this is a literal account of how our world will end. The author of the Book of Revelation scribed his dreams as allegories for enlightenment. We have misread them as literal prophecies. Now we are ensnared in their net. When mythical content leaves the realm of symbolism, it falls from grace and loses its meaning. A myth cast in stone is sterile; its mysteries cannot heal. When metaphor becomes fact, spirit dies. Literalism and inerrancy entrap, offering no escape. They are a tomb of our own making. We must roll away the stone to experience resurrection

Rigid doomsday scenarios are not limited to Western minds. Other Middle Eastern religions have a mirror image of this tale ending with equal devastation. These shared views are internalized self-hatred projected onto each other. We name our enemies and they become our evil twin. We are bent on destroying our sibling to save ourselves. Fascinated with this morbid conclusion, we rush toward self-destruction, as if acting under divine authority. We are moths flying into a flame. There is only one source of such devastating evil. Welling up from crevices deep in our unconscious mind, this hatred appears as an endless source of satanic self-loathing. There is no better way to punish an errant child who refuses life's greatest gift than to weigh him down with beliefs of everlasting damnation. Give this truant an unconscious preoccupation with horrific forecasts, burning infernos, famines, war and pestilence. These prophecies await judgment day as he hangs, suffering in the balance.

Why are we obsessed with signs of "End Times?" Consider these current events: as a culture we waste resources making war rather than looking at what festers inside. Our modern-day crusades march to destroy an outer image of wickedness we have collectively projected onto those we fear. The Y2K fiasco, in reality, was only a high-tech Armageddon; it failed. We have elected leaders who bankrupt us both monetarily and spiritually with foolery and war. These are truly signs of "End Times." They foretell a dismal finale.

Dissociation from the Spirit

Intelligent theologians debate the second coming of a Messiah to reign for a thousand years, leading forces of good against the evil ones. Again, this is the mindset of those who sought a military strategist to defeat the Romans two millennium ago. We, too, are looking for a military leader to champion forces of good against evil. This is our focal point and common belief about the Apocalyptic Myth: The Messiah will return to defeat the evil ones. Christians, Muslims and Jews all await the same arrival to lead their forces at Armageddon. We look for a righteous warrior, not a Savior, to initiate personal change. This is our ancient mistake – made again – without discussion. But our enemies are not warriors without; they are thoughts within. This need not be.

Thoughts lead to symbols as well. Mesmerized with fear, we are attempting to find an external source of evil on which to foist our mental suffering. We spend our human and natural resources to seek and destroy an antichrist, while chaos manifests in new forms. Consider these: African famines, tsunamis, hurricanes, swine flu, earthquakes and the AIDs pandemic. All result from a hidden terror. We see these as signs of the "End Times." In reality, we fashioned these horrors to castigate ourselves, as if punishing an unrepentant sinner.

Our "End Times' "devastation does not stem from a god who banishes his errant children. Rather, these hideous calamities protect us from our greatest fear; we are bent on destroying all we have rather than experience that which we unknowingly seek.

What awaits us behind this unconscious veil of terror now posing as our tragic nightmare? More flagrant than death, our bodies tremble near its presence. We go to any length rather than experience that which seeks us. Receiving such a gift becomes our greatest fear. We will destroy ourselves, while divine forgiveness patiently waits in our minds. This is the treasure for which we have searched, but it is a gift we ignore. Forgiveness, in this context, is not a pardon for wrongs done or good deeds not done. Rather, it is acknowledgement of our true spiritual nature. This is a physical body now seen as a temple of the Spirit ... a mind now containing a saved Soul. The brother in front of us becomes our mirror of Divinity; he reflects healing light for our eyes to behold.

Craving the Love of God

All that we crave waits patiently to fill our hearts. Given by our Creator before any idea of separation occurred, we seek God's unconditional love; this is first cause. We hear this as an ancient melody singing only to our heart. This is healing unguent to soothe a seething soul. It awaits an invitation to enlighten our conscious minds. This is the gift already given, the child born of an immaculate conception.

How do we avoid what so patiently seeks us? It would appear impossible to ignore treasure resting under our feet. Dissociation is the ploy. So great is our fear of God's love, we split off any such idea in our minds, rejecting the possibility of acceptance. A scapegoat is needed on which to blame this rejection of Self. He appears at the next turn. Yes, him ... he will do. Our fear becomes resentment, then hatred. Retribution is needed; someone must suffer for our pain. A preemptive strike will ease the agony of alienation. Any justification will warrant an assault. Our internal terror is now unbearable.

This is cultural dissociation, a mass psychological state or condition in which certain thoughts, emotions, sensations or memories are separated from the rest of the mind. We have separated in our minds the knowledge of God's unconditional love, then compartmentalized it with our decision to never look at the choice we have made. This is our unsacred vow of marriage. What man has put together in an unholy union, God cannot tear asunder. He is the parent overwrought with grief, watching useless suffering by his children. He weeps.

"Dissociation, the compartmentalization of experience, identity, memory, perception, and motor function, challenges many comfortable assumptions. Dissociative phenomena are often stark, extreme, and vivid. Memory for an entire period of time during which one was conscious seems lost. Identities shift between apparent opposites. Pain is ignored. Trauma victims transform the experience and report floating above their injured bodies." David Spiegel, MD

Refusing the Love of God

Why choose a belief in separation from God's most precious gift? As our greatest terror, we now refuse to look upon this unreality. Our decision for separation has been made. As our mortal sin and greatest error, do we merit self-punishment of an apocalyptic nightmare, replete with everlasting damnation? God does know of our suffering, but he does not know of this dream of separation. It is only an illusion in *our* mind.

Finding fault and blame are ancient ruses. Did not Adam blame Eve? We blame as individuals, as families, in social groups and as nations. Stopping dissociation is near impossible; stopping the denial of our true motivation is not. Just as individuals project unconscious fear outward, so do collective minds. Fixed in this grip of denial, we take extreme measures to avoid responsibility for our real motives. Unconscious fear embodies tremendous mental energy. When energy becomes trapped and bound up in our denial, it releases like a sling shot. Consequences are tragic; they rebound in drastic manners. Individuals commit mayhem and murder, cultures commit war and holocaust. Attackers and their innocent victims are bewildered and confused. Our internal fears become our external hell. The consequences for individuals are traumatic. For cultures, they become apocalyptic. We need another way to see this forecast of Armageddon.

We are Addicted and "In Denial"

Our denial appears in many forms. More subtle, yet with consequences just as tragic, are mental and physical addictions. Consider our insatiable obsession with drugs, both legal and illegal. We in the United States are without doubt major patrons of both. According to the World Health Organization (WHO), North Americans are the largest consumers of cocaine, save for the producing countries in South American (where they have chewed coca leaves for centuries). WHO reports the use of heroin and other opiates has more than tripled since 1985. Substance-abuse and treatment professionals tell us drug use – whether legal, such as prescription meds and alcohol, or illegal, such as cocaine and heroin – are only symptomatic of an underlying problem.

This hidden cause does not go away by stopping an addiction. Consider what happens if you sober up a drunken horse thief. You now have a sober horse thief. Our cultural addiction to drugs is a means for deadening the pain; we hide knowledge of our mental choice to separate from the Spirit within. This is the Christ-Self which has never left our unconscious mind. Our pain of separation is so great we need a drug to deaden the misery. Meanwhile, libations bolster courage to fight wars of conquest. We must conquer the evil one projected onto our brother's face. Drunken self-righteousness sustains our courage to wage holy wars. No wonder God weeps.

Our solution to the addiction: declare war on drugs. Appoint a drug czar. Just say no. Bent on destroying suppliers, we give little thought to cause. The villains in this drama are the drug lords in Columbia and poppy seed farmers in Thailand and Afghanistan. If we eradicate the supplier, we will satisfy our cravings. By blaming our addiction on a drug cartel, we dampen the pain within. This is the thief blaming the horse. No wonder we need ether to blot our memory. There is a primary cause for this insatiable appetite; it is our cry for spiritual renewal.

Metaphorical Discernment

Metaphorical discernment is a phrase that can be used to express, in a symbolic way, underlying causes of mental and physical addictions. As referenced earlier, substance abuse is only a symptom of a deeper problem of much greater need. This concept assumes our real desire, or reason for obsession, is mental and that each of us seeks spiritual union with an ultimate Divinity, of which we are now experientially unaware. This is Self-realization. Addictions keep us in continuous preoccupation, satisfying our cravings at a physical level so that we never question our greater mental, emotional and spiritual needs. When addictions are viewed from a metaphorical perspective, the hidden malady becomes evident. Stated another way, the addiction is an outward manifestation of an inner desire attempting to express itself. It seeks our undivided attention.

As previously referenced, an eating disorder or insatiable craving for food can be discerned as an attempt to satisfy the hunger for God. Anorexia becomes refusal to accept nourishment of the spirit. Smoking can be understood as our attempt to rekindle an extinguished flame or the eternal light within. Sexual addiction becomes an internal desire for intimacy with our Divinity. Drug addiction becomes a means of deadening the pain of separation at the conscious level. This is an attempt to raise souls in spiritual union at a "higher" realm, e.g., "getting high." Physical and mental addictions, when discerned through the eyes of the metaphoric spirit, take on new meaning. Our dark histories now become sources of light, illuminating a pathway to recovery. This perspective doesn't excuse offensive behavior; it offers a new understanding. This is self "forgiveness" in practice.

Cultural Insanity Driven by Fear

More pervasive are types of obsessions which draw upon cultural and historical phenomenon to enable addictions that fuel mass denial. Justifications are so engrained that metaphorical perspectives cannot be approached, even by rational parties seeking a mature discussion. Conversation turns to debate, and then outrage. As with individuals, attempts to curtail addictions may prompt the binge use of substances, such as a three-day drunken spree. Intervention and confinement to an institution would be the prescription. Otherwise, addicts become suicidal. If this is so for individuals, how do we respond to cultures engrossed in binge addictions and obsessed with self-destruction? We can point to militaristic regimes that destroyed entire civilizations. Consider ethnic cleansing within the last century. Entire villages were destroyed, diverting critical resources from war effort. These tactical errors were insane from a strategic military perspective, yet there was no professional or public outrage to end the slaughter ... only denial.

Let us look at an issue even closer to home, yet equally as controversial. Consider this example that polarizes our society: gun ownership. Studies by the World Rank Research Team found that 29 percent of all U.S. households own at least one handgun. This compares to seven percent in Switzerland, the next closest country. Great Britain has a one percent ownership rate. We have 5.28 handgun murders per 100,000 members of the population, compared to 1.42 by the Swiss (CIA World Handbook). Why are we obsessed with such security needs?

In all fairness, some Americans do own arms for hunting game. Others seek collector's items and many enjoy the sheer pleasure of target shooting. Gun ownership is as much a part of our current heritage as is "One Nation under God." However, for this purpose, let's look at those with a .45 under the car seat or a .38 in the night stand by the bed. This is not pleasure shooting, but an antidote for our paralyzing fear of assault and robbery. The western saga of the holstered gun and our urban myth of the "great equalizer" satisfy a need of tremendous proportions. It was Moses himself, in the guise of Charlton Heston, who taunted any would-be disarming effort with a telling statement: if you want to take my rifle from me, Heston said, you will have to "pry it from my cold dead hands."

No gun will protect us from mental attacks of baseless fears. Quite the contrary, households with guns have the highest rates of accidental shootings of family members. Gun-related suicides are at rates five times higher in homes with guns rather than those without. In reality, our risk of accidental injury and death far outweigh any apparent protection offered by firearm. What do discerning eyes see as the underlying cause for the need to appease our fear of attack, real or imagined? What hidden fear is so pervasive that we resign to shooting family and ourselves, rather than give up instruments of condemnation?

Like a dictator, we forge weapons of mass destruction to kill others in the name of protecting ourselves. We live in the most advanced of cultures, seeing ourselves as heirs to a religious heritage of love and forgiveness. Meanwhile, we beat our plowshares into swords. We could use these resources to care for the sick or feed the starving. Fear drives us to choose another way. If you find this discussion uncomfortable or offensive, then I have made my point. This is an issue that divides us so deeply. We cannot have an unheated dialogue, but only outrage. Why such polarization?

There must be an unseen cause for diversions of critical resources so apparent to sane minds. Perhaps we need protection from our unconscious fear of a false and vengeful god we created with our egos. This is a capricious deity who sacrifices small children with equal dispatch, as if they were convicted felons. He is the god of our egos who casts immutable laws in stone, then sends his chosen ones to wander in the desert for forty years. We speak of a god who would sacrifice his own son, then condemn his followers to eat his flesh and drink his blood on a weekly basis thereafter. And if that's not enough, this god ends his holy book with an awful tale of death and worldly destruction. Any who survive this chaos will endure endless waits for a final judgment day. Would shooting be too good for such a fickle god, created by our ego minds? This smaller god of our egos, we made in our minds to protect us from the love of a God who blesses our relationships, enveloping them in His wings of everlasting love. This is the God of forgiveness.

Fear of God Cuts Deep Into the Fabric of Our Society

Like Yahweh of the Old Testament or St. Paul's god of the New Testament, these are deities we praise in public, yet curse in the privacy of our unconscious. This is not God as prescribed by the author of "A Course in Miracles," nor is it a loving Father who stands patiently waiting for us at the "end of time." The former engenders fear and shame, the latter understands only unconditional love. Like Job, we need to find our God of forgiveness. The god we have created with our ego minds is raining terror. "ACIM" suggest our smaller self, the ego, has created its own image of a god that is not real. This is the god we blame for the punishment we experience in our own lives. We harbor a smoldering hatred for this punishing god in our unconscious minds. This ember bursts out in flames of self hatred, searing ourselves and all those near. This false god – the one we made in our ego mind – is causing suicidal depressions, all neatly wrapped in justifiable fratricide. This is a god we should curse and let die. We must reconsider our image of such a lesser god. We must ask to see this ego-self made image of a punishing god differently.

Consider the guilt of a child carrying death wishes for his parents. He becomes unpardonable. This is the child who cuts deeply to mutilate himself as his shame becomes unbearable. Self hatred demands retribution. So we punish ourselves with an impossible story to reinforce our guilt and hatred. This is the story we created from the Book of Revelation: the Myth of the Apocalypse! We wrote a tale so horrific no one can imagine survival, save 144,000. Now we fix it as inerrant and literal truth cast in stone. We obsess over "jots and tittles," grasping to understand its meaning. Our thinking is dazed from the thundering gallops of four horsemen racing through our minds. They foretell of burning infernos, starvation, pestilence and never-ending wars.

We (as Divine Spirits) scribed the Apocalypse, The Last Judgment and the End of Time as our myth to awaken. This is our pathway home. When fixed as literal and inerrant fact, it lost blessing of the Spirit. Discerned in a new light, we see that our Myth becomes a vehicle for projecting these horrendous fears into the collective minds. This becomes our "War on Terror." When the Book of Revelation is viewed as literal prophecy, it no longer points us to the underlying desire for which it was intended. As myth, the value of the prophecy lies in awakening us to the Christ-Self, now coming into conscious awareness. We have turned its meaning upside down. Now it becomes a literal means of destruction, which many of us cannot reconsider. The attraction is too strong. Rather than look at what we have made with our minds, it is easier to project this fear onto a faceless terrorist whose beliefs appear opposite our own. His becomes the face of an antichrist.

No drug can anesthetize the source of our pain, no gun will protect us from projections of this hidden fear. We kill one terrorist and another appears. Ideas graven in our mind will not go away. Destroying bodies will not appease the fear hidden inside. We have vowed to never let go of this miserable tale until someone "pries it from our cold dead hands."

These extreme measures suggest a homicidal manic. We intoxicate ourselves to elude our guilt. Our drunken killing spree, in the name of holy war, shrouds the shame we bear for denying our Christ-Self. Paralysis protects us from awakening to its unreality. These insane reactions are temporary measures, forestalling a dramatic change. Fortunately, our vision of horror is not an end. It is the beginning of our collective rebirth. It is a nightmare, not reality.

Christ Coming Again

A greater spiritual identity is evolving into our awareness. It is emerging from the collective unconscious into our individual conscious mind. As our greater Christ-Self moves from theoretical to experiential, it causes labor pains. Our denial and fears express themselves as cataclysmic events. Fortunately, they position us for the delivery of our true spiritual identity. We make ready for a beloved presence, an awakening for all mankind. As a bundle of joy, this is our true Second Coming.

Fear is our deadliest peril. Eradication of fear is the function of miracle workers. Exposing sources of apocalyptic fiction purges unconscious minds of paralyzing terror. Given a means for gentle awakening, we will see beyond our fixations on "End Times." Fear awaits safe removal. The outcome is certain once the process begins. This is the awakening to our Christ-Self. It is our fear espoused by the smaller or ego-self that is coming to an end. It is our fear of awakening to our Divinity that will experience "end times."

Our "last judgment" is a personal decision to move beyond fear of awakening. Rebirth is inevitable; our term of pain and suffering are only temporary. Temptation forestalls personal rapture. Cast your eyes upon a vision of freedom. When fear appears say, "Get thee behind me Satan!" We need do nothing more. Apocalyptic reign need not be. This is an unreal devil, welling up in our mind.

This journey to freedom begins for us now. An internal voice calls ... be still, listen and learn of another way to look at our apocalyptic terror. Our fear of "end times" is unwarranted. A dream to enlighten need not be graven in nightmares. Question this fear and the doors to awakening will swing open. Be willing to learn of "another way" to look at the End of Time.

What could veil our emerging spiritual identity? Movement from unconscious to conscious awareness appears a transition worse than death. Looking beyond is our key to survival. Finding support is our surest means of success. When two or more gather to look upon fear, it will not stand the light of day. This function is our personal responsibility; we must join in a "great crusade." A "holy war" must be declared on this fear; there is another way. Our end to fears of Armageddon is near. We seek a vision beyond Heaven's gate. This is spiritual vision. It has eyes of the spirit. Please ask for another way of looking at this myth of fear.

"A Course in Miracles"

One "other way" of looking at unconscious fear appeared in 1965. Dr. Helen Schucman and Dr. William Thetford questioned their work conflicts at Columbia University's College of Physicians and Surgeons in New York City. They jointly asked to see "another way" to look at the constant turmoil they experienced at work. This unsuspecting prayer triggered release of a plan to eradicate fear. It also gave us a new way to look at our obsessions with "end times" phenomena. This new way of looking at the Book of Revelation came in the form of redefining the terms which are traditionally associated with the Myth of the Apocalypse and the End of Time.

Through Dr. Schucman and Dr. Thetford's efforts came "*A Course in Miracles.*" It plots a pathway from fear to freedom. It is a stairway ascending to peace of mind. Here is an important lesson:

Our fear of "End Times" is unfounded.

A plan for restoration of sanity and a pathway to forgiveness is unfolding. We need to open our minds to its message; this is our condition precedent to understanding. It is not difficult; we have ears to hear and eyes to see. Only a small amount of "willingness" is required to trigger this release. It waits in all minds; questioning will swing open its door. It is always available to those who seek. Only be still and listen; an internal voice will thunder in this space of silence.

This guide and "*A Course in Miracles,*" is a textbook for learning. It may also become a manual for teaching. This is reassurance for those who undertake healing within themselves, their families, their communities and this world. A desire will emerge to share our newfound freedom from fear, accompanied by a welcomed message. Each of us will be given purpose and meaning extending beyond personal gain. Happiness and joy will always fill fear's void. Sharing with others strengthens resolve. Teaching will become a focus. We replace fear with an inner peace that cannot be eluded.

There is no greater vocation.

Skepticism is expected. Resistance to God's gift of self-love is deeply seated. Our internal voice calling for renewal is faint. Studying with others to question fear and attack ideas will bring them into our conscious awareness. Specific methods will be given on engaging this internal voice and looking upon our fear. The terror of looking within and questioning our true motives becomes tolerable in the presence of our friends. This gives new meaning to "bearing witness" to the spirit. Fear cannot join a union created for a holy purpose.

Each of us has a mission. Recovery from terror's plague has begun. Accepting our place in a plan to salvage our future becomes an assurance that sanity is being restored to an insane world. An awakening is well underway. Thoughts of fear are pestilences, their life cycle short. They perish with the light. Thundering hooves of apocalyptic horsemen will silence in our mind; they are aberrations. Our craving for spiritual renewal is not a famine; there is bounty to satisfy our gnawing hunger. Gather as we set a table for communion. Forgiveness will quench our thirst, peace of mind with nourish our Soul. And for the Spirit within, we will hunger no more.

A Circle of Forgiveness

Salvation awaits our willingness to rethink mistaken perceptions about the Apocalyptic Myth. We do this as we become willing to see the innocence in our brothers through the Vision of the Spiritual Eye. Another way is to study and facilitate groups whose purpose is to look at these misperceptions in our mind. This is a transformational experience we should not miss. When two or more come together for a spiritual purpose of "unlearning," something miraculous happens. Unlearning is the art of reconsidering decisions made in our minds about ourselves and others. A circle dedicated to forgiveness becomes more than a vehicle for learning; it becomes a forum to reconsider and discuss decisions upon which we do not want to look. Our egos will tell us the last place to find what we seek is in our own mind – by forgiving others.

Minds united in a holy purpose become a portal for God's love. It flows unabated from unconscious to conscious minds. Fear in our ego mind will resist love's flow. When joined in a circle, it has no opposition. Forgiveness surges over and around our fears, illuminating their unreality. Collective change occurs as individuals, joined together, question fear-based thoughts. It takes only a few to get started. Remember, we are the critical few.

Forgiveness as prescribed by the Voice or of "A Course in Miracles" has eluded many traditional Western religions. It is easy to see evil in another. It shines like a beacon in darkness. Foreign evildoers are easy targets to Western minds. We can readily point to institutional wrongs. A loving God could not permit inhuman atrocities on such vast scales. Very simply, He did not. Consider this proposition: our nation erupted in a Civil War over the institutions of slavery and state's rights. Family members fought each other, so deeply held were our feelings. Lives and resources were wasted beyond imagination. We sued for peace only after total destruction. Many religious and social institutions supported this destruction and carnage. Had every member of every church refused to participate, could war have taken place? Our inherent moral belief system produces the results before us, whether we consciously subscribe to them or not. Evil is a false belief that starts within. When messages of forgiveness are contaminated with political, social and moral agendas, they lose the healing power of the Spirit. Fortunately, a correction dictated to Drs. Thetford and Schucman reintroduces a message of divine love when we become willing to offer forgiveness.

Our Children as Assassins in Schoolyards

If our collective thought system is convinced this world will end in burning infernos, then it will. If these thoughts reflect our conscious and unconscious beliefs, we will make them happen. Natural disasters aside, adequate modes of mass destruction are in arsenals around our planet today. Using weapons to appease our fear of attack is a collective thought system in our unconscious minds; it must be exposed and acknowledged. A little willingness is the ability to stop denying our unwillingness. We must choose again.

Self-loathing harbored in our unconscious mind is projected upon those we judge to be evil in our world. They become targets of mass destruction. Even a novice studying self-awareness understands this principle: an attack on another will have an equally dramatic mental impact on us. Eradicating evildoers will not remove self-hatred in our mind. These obscene acts rebound in our face. What goes around, comes back around. This is our Western version of karmic law.

As more children become suicidal assassins in our schoolyards, we continue to cry in bewilderment, "why?" Are they acting out unconscious fear and shame we have let loose on ourselves and others? Do children as murderers assume our "collective" projection of self-effacement and mutilation, and then make it personal? In this respect, the sins of parents are visited on their children. If this is collateral damage from our projection of evil outward, it now flies in our faces. We cannot bomb innocent civilians on one side of the globe without expecting self-retribution on the other. The ego's collective mind has a global reach.

Fortunately, these acts of desperation also bear our message of salvation. Sacrificial children become our saviors awaiting rebirth. Like swords of Herod, our egos seek to kill this new born Christ child within. It goes deeper into Egypt, hiding in the unconscious. Waiting, it seeks ears to hear and eyes to see our message of forgiveness. Children as assassins bear a message of desperation, rebirth and, finally, resurrection. It is our fear-based thought system, obsessed with self-destruction, which must be crucified. The Peace of God will resurrect as our Christ-Self; it will dominate thought in our minds. This is our gift of forgiveness. This is the true "Second Coming." When we silence the punishing guns of violence in our own minds, this will become our experience – first here, then around our world.

Changing Our Mind about the World

"*A Course in Miracles*" central theme hinges on this reality: we cannot change the world, but we can change our minds about the world. This process starts by becoming conscious of attack thoughts in our own mind. It concludes with re-evaluating our decisions to choose these thoughts. We must "choose again." Becoming willing to change our thoughts will change the images we project outward upon our fellows. An option to "choose again" can be made at any time. We can supplant attack thoughts with thoughts of forgiveness. We do this "in time," which is the miracle. Unfortunately, time is wasting. To reiterate, the purpose of this text is to offer a study guide introducing this message:

Our fears about the "End of Time" are unfounded.

As each of us begins to study a message of forgiveness, God's plan for restoration of peace will unfold. Accepting realities of this truth will accelerate awareness in conscious minds. As rates of change increase, the accelerated transformation, or "Speed-Up," begins. The love of God stands at the "end of time." Fear exists only in time. It prevails between us and Heaven. Neither fear nor time is reality; they appear as obstacles of our own making. They must be given to this Spirit of forgiveness in our mind. These thoughts become teachers, our maximal learning experiences. God's hands are always extended, offering forgiveness. We have no need to fear. It is our old "concepts" of time that are coming to an end. This is the real meaning of "The End of Time."

A decision for forgiveness has already been made in our unconscious mind. We each are called to become a teacher of God. We teach by practicing. A "Circle of Forgiveness" offers an invitation to join in communion with each other. This is a table set to serve forgiveness. Healing takes place by extending through our minds. It transforms both sender and receiver. This is cause and effect in proper use. Love set free comes round again and again. What we seek now seeks us. This, too, is karmic law.

If we are to be reborn, we must become teachable, as if little children. This means offering willingness to release old concepts. Like a patient midwife, an internal Teacher waits in our mind, ready to assist when we offer the "little willingness" to change our thinking.

One such idea is our concept of the hereafter. As an integral part of the Apocalyptic Myth, we need to revisit our concept of Heaven. We must know where we are going if we are to know when we arrive. John Burroughs said it best, "The Kingdom of Heaven is not a place, but a state of mind." Fortunately, we have hidden it within.

Choosing a Mind Full of Heaven

If Heaven is the ultimate destination, how do we get there? "*ACIM*" offers a new perspective on the nature of Heaven. Celestial means Heaven, and all heavenly bodies. Not just outer bodies like planets or stars, but also inner bodies such as mental energy. These are thoughts held in mind. Celestial is a place of peace, a space absent of conflict. As thought and experience, we hold these ideas individually and collectively.

All religions tell of life after death. Great spiritual teachers experienced the hereafter. Jesus, founder of Christianity, went to prepare such a place. Buddha experienced Nirvana after enlightenment. Krishna speaks of inner purity which strengthens consciousness, and then sorrow disappears. Is this Heaven? Muhammad returned from his night journey promising rewards for faithful followers in Heaven. Lao Tzu, scribe of Taoism, tells of a world beyond the 10,000 myriad things: the real world. These teachers did not die to experience the hereafter. Each received understanding in a unique way: through revelation.

Knowledge of Heaven is older than time. Having never left our unconscious mind, it patiently awaits recall. We choose not to remember our place in Heaven. Fortunately, a new message has been given. It is as if Christianity's founder returned and corrected misperceptions in his original teachings by channeling them to Dr.

Schucman with the help of Dr. Thetford while they taught at Columbia University's Medical School.

The two professors were asked to impart this knowledge as their function in the current "Celestial Speed-Up." This came as a great surprise to Bill Thetford and Helen Schucman. They were perplexed by the request. Their knowledge of the psyche supported by a curious nature led them to do as the author instructed, taking notes for "A Course in Miracles." He gave specific answers about the nature of Heaven, advising it already exists in our minds. We may experience this awareness now in the form of peace, contentment, happiness and joy. Unfortunately, these thoughts reside beyond grasp of our conscious minds. We are preoccupied with our body and brain.

We have the freedom to experience Heaven as a Celestial sphere of thought because it is already in our mind. All great spiritual teachers understood this lesson and shared their memories of Heaven. Doctrines vary, but upon leaving confinement to the idea of being only a body, they received a glimpse of the life hereafter. So powerful was their experience, each came back to tell of Heaven's realms. In the Buddhist tradition, these are the Bodhisattvas – the enlightened ones who returned to teach others. We benefit from their experience, avoiding travails in space and time. A spiritual teacher shortens time.

An Idea Whose Time Has Come

An idea "whose time has come" receives general acceptance in our minds. Collective awareness is more than literal understanding; it is a deep and profound truth. Uncommon knowledge is now common among equals. The Greeks call this gnosis – the experiential knowledge. This truth's nature is not subject to interpretation or change, but is understood. Understanding need not be verbal. Those who understand know. Great spiritual teachers share knowledge in this manner. Being in their presence brings forth the experience. Learning from someone's experience is a time-saving device. Time collapses in their presence.

Collapsing time is a means of acceleration. Accepting an awareness of another's experience of Heaven brings reality closer in time and space. Heavenly bodies are permanent ideas of peace in our mind. Healing is the acknowledgement they already exist. This is how great spiritual teachers heal. They bring into our conscious awareness an idea already in our unconscious mind. Spiritual healing occurs first in our mind. In an instant, a tiny gap between knowledge and experience is closed. We have an internal Teacher who will help us bridge this gap. Healing of our mind may manifest in our bodies. Sometimes it may not.

Resistance to the idea of Heaven, or healing, fogs this gap in our minds. Awareness of this resistance is the first step in its removal. Nothing else need be done to begin the experience or thought of Heaven. This is the beginning of spiritual healing. Acknowledging our defiance weakens death's grip of denial on the experience of Heaven. By definition, acknowledging this unwillingness becomes our "little willingness." We need do nothing more, only become willing to acknowledge the denial of our unwillingness which clouds this tiny gap. Heaven becomes our experience in the form of healing of our minds.

The Tube

London's subway system – the Tube – is an excellent means of rapid travel. Arriving trains are welcomed by a pre-recorded warning. Those exiting cars must beware of uneven levels and open spaces between trains and station deck. A recorded voice advises, "Mind the gap." For an American, this is an odd choice of words. In a way, it is a reminder of this tiny gap in our mind. This is the narrow void separating Heaven and self-damnation

Nothing else need be done to remove our resistance, just "mind the gap." The voice for truth, our chosen spiritual Teacher, is already in our mind. It takes our acknowledgement and combines it with the Spiritual Eye's perfect knowledge. The gap is bridged. We only need be aware of denial or remember the tiny gap in our unconsciousness mind. Resistance to this idea is strong; do not fight denial. When two or more join together and share their "little willingness," resistance to knowledge of Heaven becomes nil. A portal through which divine love flows opens in this absence of conflict and fills the gap. It enters our conscious awareness. This is how "knowing" or knowledge becomes collective.

Shared knowledge of our denial of "unwillingness" must become greater than our joint resistance for a shift to occur. When our choice for peace becomes collective, the "Celestial Speed-Up" occurs. This is Earth now functioning in Heaven's awareness. This has already happened in our minds. It awaits our key to unlock a new understanding. Just "mind the gap." Time stands still. We will experience peace of mind, a promise from the author of "*A Course in Miracles*." As it begins to happen for each of us, it will begin to happen for us all. .

Unlearning Our Myth of Apocalypse

The Book of Revelation contains a path to self-realization which will awaken the individuated Christ-Self in each of us. This is the journey we have begun, awakening the Christ-Self within. The first step is unlearning or reconsidering the myths of condemnation and self destruction we have created about ourselves and our fellows – particularly the ones we call evil enemies. Our protagonists contain the key to our awakening. We must rely on them. As long as we condemn those we call evil and antichrists, they block our awakening and serve as a barrier to initiating the Second Coming.

We must reconsider these myths in our mind. Time itself is the first. Miracles happen "in time." They also suspend time. When time stops, we experience the reality of Heaven's peace in our mind. As we change our way of thinking about time, ourselves and others, the miracle occurs. A miracle changes our mind; we see from a new perspective. This is vision from the Spiritual Eye. When our minds change, a new reality opens before us.

We must rethink the "End of Time." How will time end? Open your mind to a new concept of time, for it is our old "concept" of time that is coming to an end.

Chapter 3

The End of Time

The Speed-Up and Time

Just as we are preoccupied with our Apocalyptic Myth, so we are mesmerized in attempts to forecast when the doom will begin and end. Dates have been set in every millennium foretelling of the day, the exact time and place. We have been functioning in "End Times" since the Garden of Eden. If we are to dispel this Myth, we must begin to question our models of time that are an integral part of these perceptions. Time is a concept we have made in our minds to keep us trapped in everlasting damnation. Time, as a constant, does not exist in the outer world. Time is a thought system we have created in our inner world on which we have come to agree. In order to free ourselves from the fear of "End of Times," we must first begin to question our entire concept of time. Correction begins in our mind, not on a clock or calendar.

The "Speed-Up" collapses time. Our new understanding of time is critical to correcting these erroneous belief systems. Time is a measure for recording events. Since we created time, we can change time to fit particular needs. We can save daylight by changing time, or we can actually save time itself. Time is fluid, not rigid. It serves the means for which we fashioned. Time can stand still, be warped or end abruptly. It even extends into infinity. These are all figures of speech, but isn't time just a figment of our imagination?

Time is like clay; it can be molded in the hands of a sculptor.

Our bodies cast a shadow on the dark side of light. A shadow has no reality; it is an outcome we see from changes in intensity or brightness. A shadow can disappear in an instant – when light returns – or fall longer until it disappears with the sun. Shadows can be used to tell time, as with a sundial. The Earth's rotations and their relationship to the sun are the basis for natural time itself. If we were born without eyes, could we comprehend natural time or see a shadow? Both are dependent upon external vision. Shadows and time are concepts we hold in our minds. They appear to measure specific needs we have created. They can appear and disappear at our behest.

In the absence of light, a shadow is no more. In the absence of time, the world we created with our egos is no more. The faulty thought system we depend upon needs "time" to exist. It is the basis for the shame, guilt and fear we experience each moment in time. We believe time is a linear progression, always marching onward. We cannot go back in time, only forward … but is this true? Do events proceed only in the same direction as does our instrument for measuring? Time always moves on … or does it stand still? We cannot travel in time, yet there are time travelers. Coming to see time as a concept we have created for a specific purposes is part of the "unlearning" process presented by *A Course in Miracles*." Learning to distinguish our thoughts and resulting events as being "in time" is a means of separating our ego thought systems' results from the Divine thought system in our mind.

Time is like a substance filling a container; it is limited to the confines of its vessel. Time will end when the thought of sin remains no more. The belief in separation exists "in time," which it needs to support its existence.

Some of you may recall a stanza from a college drinking song: "In Heaven there is no beer, that's why we drink it here." Well, in Heaven there is no time. If we cling to an erroneous belief that time is a firm reality and not a figment of our imagination, we are excluding ourselves from the thought of Heaven. We must choose where we wish to be: in time or in eternity. Do we want Heaven and peace of mind, or the ego thought system which we have made "in time."

Apocalyptic thinking hinges on events happening "in time." We must understand how this world and our understanding of time will end. We have made this belief that time is real and must end in death and destruction. Our fear of "End Times" is symptomatic of looking upon this unholy union. It tells us not to look upon what we have made in conjunction with our egos, lest we vanish into a burning inferno. In the absence of "time" there is "timelessness."

God stands patiently at the "end of time" awaiting our decision. Joining with the spiritual Teacher in our mind is a decision to stand with God, not stand in time. We do not need to suffer this belief of separation in time for one moment longer. The decision for God begins by questioning an unshakeable belief in our minds: that this world is coming to an abrupt end. But it is our *concept* of time that is coming to an end, not the world itself. This is a correction of our apocalyptic fallacy. In Heaven is only timelessness.

Saving time is a central focus of this Celestial Speed-Up. The actual "unlearning" of our inherent belief "in time" is the function of a spiritual Teacher in our minds. We created time for a purpose. It was intended to keep us entombed in an everlasting belief of separation until we become willing to see its true purpose. Offer only the "little willingness." We do this by becoming willing to stop denying our unwillingness. This begins the unlearning process. Free from our erroneous thinking, we in turn give permission to our chosen spiritual Teacher to use these old concepts of time as a means for awaking. Time takes on a holy purpose. A new understanding of time awaits us now.

This is the reality of our fear about the "end of time."

The Other Way

This correction of time and redefinition of forgiveness began anew with the scribing of "*ACIM.*" Dr. Helen Schucman and Dr. Bill Thetford asked for a new way to look at the frustrations they were experiencing at Columbia University. Their request for restoration was answered. Dr. Helen Schucman began to have disturbing dreams. After a period of unrest and confusion, she discussed her visions with Dr. Thetford, head of the department. He suggested she not resist the experiences, but share them with him at the Medical School. Reluctantly, she agreed. What came next was an internal awareness appearing as an intuitive voice. It instructed her to take dictation.

"Please take notes this is A Course in Miracles". So began the Text.

At Bill's insistence, she took messages in shorthand. Each day, Helen would bring her steno pad to his office. After locking the door, Bill would type the messages she had transcribed. What unfolded over the next 10 years was "*A Course in Miracles,*" consisting of a 600 plus-page text. Also transcribed: a *"Manual for Teachers"* and a *"Workbook for Students,"* the latter consisting of 365 daily lessons. . These three books comprise current published editions of *"A Course in Miracles."* All gave new meaning to miracles which happen "outside of time."

This internal voice dictated to Helen a very new understanding of key components within Christianity's message. It included a fresh look at the Book of Revelation, the Apocalypse, the Last Judgment and the "End of Time." This message is entirely antithetical to fear-baiting beliefs espoused in apocalyptic books and movies. It counters messages of shame and guilt shouted from religious pulpits. It also dispels our myth of doomsday scenarios that deliver a fiery end to our world.

A re-definition of God's "chosen ones" was given. It tells us who will experience the Rapture. This account is absence of fear offering a vision of gentle awakening to a renewed awareness of God's love. Assuring us forgiveness is already in our minds, it suggests our terror projected onto the "End Times" phenomenon is really our fear of God's love. Promising to see beyond these obstacles, the *Course*'s author details how we will awaken to a new reality of our Divine relationship. As our concept of time comes to an end, we will have a new awareness of the Second Coming. Our needless fears of awakening to this reality will no longer manifest in apocalyptic nightmares. This was their new message about Revelation.

Helen and Bill shared one of their original manuscripts with the Association for Research and Enlightenment (A.R.E.) in Virginia Beach, Va. This edition became known as the Hugh Lynn Cayce (HLC) Version. Most know of A.R.E. as the foundation started by Hugh Lynn's father, Edgar Cayce. As a 20th Century mystic, the elder Cayce is most famous for his prophecies. His predictions came with great surprise; he was responding to questions while in a trance. The elder Cayce could read the individualized unconscious mind of his patients. Cayce's teachings on metaphysics came from a place of higher learning deep in the unconscious. While some made light of his work, Cayce was actually invited to the White House to give his readings to President Woodrow Wilson. Unfortunately for Wilson, he advised the president of the difficulties he would experience from his current illness. He also predicted the League of Nations would not be approved by Congress. Both visions came true. Like Helen, Cayce was reluctant to engage these psychic experiences; he thought them more insanity than divinity. Since both their communications have withstood tests of time, we need to listen for their ring of truth.

Bill Thetford was intrigued with the writings and work of the elder Cayce. As a student of parapsychology and channeling, he pursed these interests at Columbia Medical College. Realizing that Helen's experiences were similar to channeled communications through Cayce, Bill arranged a meeting with the younger Cayce to seek his advice. Helen reluctantly agreed to visit A.R.E and discuss their Text. Fortunately, Hugh Lynn Cayce gave Helen needed reassurance to validate the message. He also raised an interesting point about the author of *"ACIM"* that became lost in the publishing process. Principally, he questioned the source of knowledge given in the Text and, more specifically, who or what were the source and how many voices dictated the materials.

The Voice for Correction

The first four chapters of the HLC version are different from the published editions of *"ACIM,"* in both content and form. The reference to a "Celestial Speed-Up" is particularly significant. This phrase was removed from the published Text at the request of Helen. She apparently thought it to be insignificant. The first chapter, entitled "Miracle Principles," defines "Celestial" as that sphere beyond physical laws where man is perfect. There are many symbols for this concept. You may think of this as a place in our Divine minds, residing beyond time. This is a space where perfection already exists, but not necessarily a physical destination. As a metaphor for our ultimate reality, this is our awareness of Heaven. It can be experienced, but not defined. This concept of Heaven may not have streets of gold, but it ensures peace of mind.

In more poetic terms, the Voice suggested we are being called to this sphere of thought by an ancient melody. It sings only to our hearts. Who is this Voice behind this message? I believe the voice which communicated with Helen and Bill is seeking to communicate with each of us as well. Hugh Lynn Cayce suggested two or more Voices dictated the Text. This would explain how language and concepts differ in the first four chapters from the remaining chapters in *"ACIM."*

One major change deals with a direct, conscious communication link to our Divine mind: our understanding of a God within. The author of the Course refers to this as the "Spiritual Eye." The editor for the published first Text chose to standardize the language throughout the entire work with Christian names and terms. It changes the significances of the first four chapters and its messages about the Apocalypse and the End of Time. Spiritual Eye is not a new name; it predates Christianity. Ancient Egyptians used this image to describe a part of our mind which sees with spiritual vision. Put another way, this is a faculty which views our world through eyes of forgiveness. This is forgiveness that is not a reprieve for a wrong done. Rather, it is a willingness to reconsider our perception of each other as more than just a physical body that is born and dies. This is our gift from the Voice "for" God.

You can see the Egyptian Spiritual Eye every day. It touches more Americans than any other spiritual symbol. The eye atop the pyramid on the dollar bill is an image of the ancient Spiritual Eye: the all-knowing, all-seeing Eye of Providence. This Egyptian symbol was adopted by the Masonic Temple. Many of our democracy's founders were Masons; their symbols are used in our important documents, emblems and structures. Masonry carries the mysteries of an ancient spirituality through ritual and symbol. Our Nation's capitol was laid out by a Frenchman, Pierre Charles L'Enfant, who served under George Washington as an officer in the Revolutionary War. Both L'Enfant and Washington were Masons. Look at an aerial image of the National Mall; it is designed after a cross. Horizontal arms spread from the White House to the Jefferson Memorial. A vertical arm extends from our Capitol to the Lincoln Memorial.

In the center of the cross is the Washington Monument, an obelisk generally accepted as a spiritual or phallic symbol of our Divinity. In many eastern religions, these sexual and spiritual symbols are one and the same. Spirituality and sexuality cannot be separated. They are opposite sides of the same coin. Who we are sexually is intrinsic to who we are spiritually. In the Western world, we cannot bear their joining. We will discuss further sexual distortions of miracles impulses in later chapters. It will suggest why sexuality is such a key aspect of our spiritual identity.

The author or voice of "*ACIM*" distinguishes himself from the voice "for" God, suggesting we refer to the author as an Elder Brother who has earned our respect. Divine love speaks in many tongues. Not everyone hears the same voice; lessons are individualized for our maximum learning experience. This Voice for truth speaks in different dialects, but the message is clear: all will learn of miracles. Only our place "in time," when we chose to start, is optional.

The Voice of the Course will be clear about its identity. It speaks for the same mind that was in Christ Jesus, founder of Christianity. Offering blessings to those miracle-minded, the Voice gives peace of mind to those who have chosen to listen to thoughts other than fear in their own minds. The miracle-minded do this by seeing fear's unreality through personalized learning experiences. Remember, our ego minds are extremely resistant to the unlearning process. When joined in a circle for this holy purpose, ego resistance becomes nil. Divine love will cleanse false concepts now clouding our mind.

All Are Called, Few Choose to Listen

Let's look at certain widely held beliefs now cornerstones of most apocalyptic thinking. For instance, only God's "chosen people" will experience the Rapture and be taken to Heaven. The voice of the Course references a Biblical verse that tells us,

> *"Many are called, but few are chosen."*

The author advises this correction,

> *"ALL are called, but few choose to listen. "*
>
> *Therefore, they do not choose RIGHT".*

The onus of choosing is in our minds, not the mind of an arbitrary God in some remote heaven. Not a message of judgment, it is a message of personal decision. The voice continues to explain "chosen ones" are merely those who choose right thinking or with the "right mind" sooner, not later. The Voice "for" God is in our right mind. We are free to choose, at any point "in time."

"*ACIM*" distinguishes between right-mindedness and wrong-mindedness. The latter, or wrong mind, is of our own making, home of the ego thought system. The former is that part of our mind which can hear the voice of the Spiritual Eye, the Voice "for" God. This is our pathway to peace of mind and happiness. When choosing to listen with our right minds, we choose correctly.

Why did such an important message go directly to doctors of teaching psychologists at the Columbia Medical College? One would think a Divine correction would come through theological sources. Bill and Helen were both analytical scientists with questioning minds. As intellectuals and professors at a top medical school and respected members of their profession, they were skeptical of being used as a channel for spiritual messages.

Reading their biographies, it becomes clear neither Bill nor Helen were motivated to change the world through correcting a spiritual teaching. They were reluctant participants. Only after repeated attempts to understand the message did they submit themselves to the task at hand. Their conscious prayer was to find a "better way" to work together. This prayer resonated deep in the unconscious, at the level of the heart. Think of "heart" not as a physical organ, rather a symbol of choosing to hear the Voice for God, the Spiritual Eye. Choosing with the heart is characterized by lack of any other option. All other avenues have been exhausted and now resistance is non-existent. A "prayer of the heart" is uttered without reservation. It is not a plea but rather, an affirmation. Their request for "another way" came immediately, with force. Even an unconscious "prayer of the heart" receives a direct answer.

Prayer's only requirement is our "little willingness" to be still and listen. "*ACIM's*" definition of willingness is our ability to stop denying our "unwillingness." This is significant; it does not require us to take action or even change our minds. Becoming conscious of our "unwillingness" is the only requirement. The Spiritual Eye or Voice for God will correct our perception. We have chosen with the right mind when we experience peace or absence of conflict in our conscious mind. It is that simple.

The Celestial Speed-Up and Our Part in the Plan

According to "*ACIM*," everyone has a part in the "Plan" of salvation. No one's participation is absent from our grand scheme of recovery. Each will become aware of a specific time and place to execute their part. When a critical number of minds join in the "prayer of the heart," miraculous things will happen. Our thoughts will transcend beyond time and space. Transformation will accelerate. We each have special talents to share. This is the real meaning of the Celestial Speed-Up. We can do this now. The sooner we make this choice, the sooner we find rest for our soul. God knows us only in peace – our true reality. We can say the Celestial Speed-Up is an increase in the rate of acceleration toward our destiny with spiritual perfection. It is a quickening in awareness, a willingness to identify with that place in our minds which lies beyond space and time.

The Speed-Up means as more choose to listen to this Voice – the Voice "for" God – everyone awakens at an accelerated rate. We literally save thousands of years "in time." Miracles collapse time because they suspend time and use a thought system outside our concept of time. Choosing correctly means we experience peace in our hearts and calm in our minds.

Mankind is on a collision course with God's Divine love. This destination is irreversible, "in time." Fortunately, time is under our control, because it is of our own making and will be used for the purposes of the Spiritual Eye – when we become willing to allow this to happen.

"*ACIM's*" author told Helen, her – and Bill's – special skills were needed for this "Speed-Up" because the world's citizens were losing more than they were gaining. Helen asked the voice why she and Bill were being chosen as scribes. It responded by telling Helen the world was in a terrible situation and needed correction. As explained by Kenneth Wapnick, Ph.D., in his book, "*Absence from Felicity*," she and Bill were being asked to take their part in a plan of helping others to change their minds more quickly. The author or Voice needed their talents on behalf of The Plan. Many people were being called back into this world to take their part in the present "Speed-Up." "*A Course in Miracles*" is only one part of The Plan.

The Plan referenced in this quote above is a Plan to choose a state of mind other than fear. It is known as the Plan of Atonement or "At-One-Ment," also called God's Plan of Salvation. The Course's author is responsible for implementing this Plan. He suggested we respond to him as if he is an elder brother who has greater experience that ourselves. Everyone has a part in God's Plan of Salvation when we chose to accept it. Atonement and salvation are given new meaning by the Text's Author. These terms have nothing to do with social or political theology; they address methods to awaken individuals to a message of forgiveness in our own minds. This awakening can be compared to the process of individuation or Self-actualization, which takes place in the higher place of learning in our unconscious mind and brings our identity as the Christ-Self to fruition.

Everyone's part in The Plan will be revealed to them when we begin to choose correctly. We know we are choosing correctly as we begin to experience peace in our mind. We experience peace when we are content to be happy, rather that right. The only requirement for assuming our part in the Atonement is offering our "little willingness" to heal our belief in separation from Divine love. The little willingness is offered when we are ready to stop denying our "unwillingness" to experience a peace-filled mind.

We Have Experienced Speed-ups Before

The Celestial Speed-Up is not a theory. It is a practical occurrence we have seen many times. What we need is a different set of eyes to discern the effects of accelerated unlearning. Here are two practical examples of "Speed-Ups" which transformed our human consciousness on a global basis. Both offered miraculous effects by healing our minds, then our bodies.

The United States in the 1950s found summer a time of fear and anxiety for parents. This was the season when children by the thousands became infected with the crippling disease poliomyelitis, or polio. Children of the 1950s remember the images of iron lungs for the severely paralyzed. These huge machines, containing human bodies withering away, were terrorizing to a child and a parent's worst nightmare. The March of Dimes was formed to raise funds for the search for a cure and to help those still afflicted.

This burden of fear was lifted immediately with the announcement Dr. Jonas Salk had developed a vaccine against the disease in 1955. Salk became world-famous overnight after his many years of painstaking research. Those who lived prior to this discovery will agree: the fear of polio was as paralyzing to our minds as it was to our bodies. Salk was hailed a miracle worker; he further endeared himself to the public by refusing to patent the vaccine. Having no desire to profit personally from his discovery, he merely wished to see the vaccine disseminated as widely as possible. That's a miracle which expressed itself by changing our minds.

Eradication of this crippling disease still continues, but freedom from this fear took effect immediately. Hope emerged in the absence of fear. Dr. Salk's "act of love" did not help those who were infected with the virus, but it did have an immediate effect on those terrorized by the fear of paralysis. In different terms, we could characterize this universal fear as a "call for love." Dr. Salk responded as a vehicle for answering this call with an "act of love." The response came in a form that we could understand, a medical remedy. Centuries of fear were instantaneously replaced with new hope. As a "Speed-Up," it created a rapid change in perception that accelerated on a global basis. The fear of polio was eradicated.

A Time-Released Speed-Up in Steps

In 1935, alcoholism in the U.S. was rampant. There were no effective remedies. In June of that year, Bill Wilson, a New York stockbroker, was introduced to Dr. Bob Smith, a physician from Columbus, Ohio. Their meeting began the modern 12 Step Movement. Unlike polio, alcoholism had an extremely negative social stigma. It was widely perceived as a societal blight afflicting only the morally degenerated. This "call for love" manifested itself differently than our fear of paralysis.

In order to overcome the shame associated with alcoholism and to protect the spirituality of its membership, recovery programs remained anonymous. The result was a "timed release" from fear. While anonymity appeared as a dampening effect in the spread of new recovery groups , it was really a loving way for our minds to heal and gently awaken to the truth. This is how Divine love expresses itself in other ways. This is how a spiritual Teacher uses time. It took 40 years for this dissemination to move into the general public's conscious awareness. Shame and guilt are toxic energies, not easily purged. As the shame associated with the disease of alcoholism was reduced, recovery accelerated.

In the spring of 1939, the fledging organization published the book *Alcoholic Anonymous*. The small recovery groups had approximately 100 members collective. It adopted the name of its book for the organization and then went from a flying blind period into a new phase of its pioneering pathway in the history of this spiritual movement. In the fall of 1939, the editor of *Liberty* magazine wrote a very favorable article entitled "Alcoholics and God." A frantic rush of 800 inquiries increased their numbers from 100 to 800 by the end of 1939.

From their own accounts in the publication *Alcoholic Anonymous*, John D. Rockefeller, Jr. gave a dinner in 1940 for many of his influential friends and AA members told their stories of recovery from alcoholism. News of the event was placed on the world wired communication system and many suffering alcoholics when to book stores to buy the book and inquires flooded into the New York tiny office for information about recovery and meeting groups to attend. By March of 1941, the number had risen to 2,000.

An article in the *Saturday Evening Post* in that same year place such a compelling picture before the public that alcoholics seeking recover deluged the organization. By the end of 1941 AA numbered over 8,000 members. They refer to the acceleration as a "mushrooming process" in full swing which boosted the group to a national institution. In their words it was a "wholesale miracle" in the way AA had grown from a meeting of two to 8,000 in a two year span with no membership solicitation, only those who chose to join. AA is a program of attraction, not promotion. By March of 1976 AA had become a worldwide institution with over 1,000,000 members in 90 countries and over 28,000 meeting groups. When two or more come together for a Holy purpose, miraculous events do happen.

Here in the USA, First Lady Betty Ford's treatment for alcoholism in 1978 opened even wider the flood gates of public awareness. During the next 10 years, recovery from alcoholism became widely accepted – and sometimes in vogue. During the 1970-80s, treatment centers sprang up across the U.S. Now in the 21st Century, alcoholism has become de-stigmatized. In 1981, there were over 42,000 groups in

110 countries. The shame associated with the disease has lessened or been removed.

During the past 40 years, the demand for treatment centers has decreased here in the USA. The primary obstacle to recovery remains denial of this disease. Medical professionals, ministers, public law officials and suffering family members suggest going to 12-step meetings as a proven means of spiritual recovery from alcoholism. One could conclude there is an inverse relationship between the reduction in shame and the rate of acceleration in recovery. My lack of math skills will not allow me to figure the exact rate of acceleration, but I am sure it's a steep curve on the chart; unknown millions have experienced recovery through working the 12-Steps of AA and finding a Higher Power on which they have come to rely.

The successful treatment of alcoholism was slow to move into public consciousness. Eliminating the fear of polio was immediate when compared to alcoholism. It took Alcoholics Anonymous approximately 50 years for its recovery process to finish its move into full public awareness. Alcoholism has been considered a social malady since wine was first fermented. In reality, public acceptance of recovery efforts has been rapid given the scope of time since grapes were first crushed, given a broader perspective.

One of the interesting characteristics of the acceleration effect came to light during the 1970s. The average age of those in recovery dropped from the 40s and 50s down to early and mid-20 to 30s. Teens are now included in recovery groups. This is the "Speed-Up" concept in practical application. As the number accepting recovery grows, the understanding and certainty of relief becomes part of our collective consciousness. This understanding is a form of "knowing." Alcoholics could find a solution by offering the "little willingness."

Knowledge at the Experiential Level

Knowledge or "knowing" is significant in understanding accelerated change. It promotes transference from the collective to individual minds. For instance, when newcomers enter AA meeting rooms, most will confirm they have accepted their drunken insanity as hopeless. Many are close to suicide. Fortunately, those already in recovery have experiences to the contrary. Their knowledge at the experiential level is closer to surety. As a rule, there is no logical attempt to dissuade newcomers of their belief in the hopelessness of recovery. Rather, members share personal accounts of individual experiences. During months of repeated exposure, this knowledge or "knowing" enters into the newcomers' conscious acceptance. The knowledge becomes inherent. This is transference, from the collective knowledge and experience of the group, to the individual. It happens every day in 12-step groups.

Most 12-step participants offer explanations of a spiritual nature as a source of change in their minds. The transference of knowledge releases them from the obsession to drink. It is the conscious joining – for a spiritual purpose – absence of conditions or demands that permits the change. When two join together for a spiritual purpose, conscious healing takes place. When many join, the effects accelerate. This is an aspect of the "prayer of the heart" referenced earlier. This is the "Speed-Up" in practice.

Recovery stories are consistent. At some point in time preceding any AA meeting, most in recovery experienced a moment of clarity, then a subsequent surrender. The language varies but is usually expressed as, "I am ready for another way. Drinking alcohol is not working anymore." What follows this awareness is directed contact, either purposeful or circumstantial, leading the alcoholic to an AA meeting. Most enter voluntarily, but some enter through jail, the courts or hospitals. There is a common thread with the stories of those who have succeeded in recovery. It appears as an unbroken chain of events and begins with a decision to seek change, usually at a point of surrender. Shortly thereafter, a contact is made for entry with attendance at meetings and finally, recovery. The restoration period may take years, but the stories are quite similar. Only time will vary. And time, as we know, is under our control.

One other significant point: Alcoholic Anonymous, Alanon and Overeaters Anonymous (OA) are the oldest and most successful of the 12-step recovery programs, compared to newer applications like Narcotics Anonymous (NA). The level of confidence and certainty of recovery in AA, Alanon and OA for newcomers appears to be significantly greater than in NA groups. The latter have less history sustaining long-term recovery. AA's continuous terms in years of sobriety are multiples of those in NA, based on casual observances.

There are many factors which could affect this condition, but one obvious reason: narcotic addiction retains a negative social stigma associated with drug abuse. Drug addiction has its criminal aspects, and the disease has toxic levels of shame. These are religiously and politically reinforced. Our internalized shame is projected onto dealers, users and abusers. They become our scapegoats. In the United States, our emphasis is on stopping drug dealers, not addressing addiction and craving. We do nothing to stop demand. A source of external shame is a convenient relief. We can project our shame on the dealers; a drug lord in South America will do. This is a cultural projection in application. Rather than examine our own motivations for addiction, we choose to see the problem in the supplier. The thief again blames the horse.

One could say the significant differences between AA and NA are in levels of conscious "knowing" recovery is not just probable, but inevitable. The "knowing" stems from the difference in term of years in recovery between the two groups; AA is much older. All that is required is the desire to stop drinking or using. This is the effect of "conscious knowing" in collective minds. The fear of addiction and fear of recovery has been replaced with hope; seasoned members know a newcomer's "call for love" will be answered. In time, transference in consciousness takes place. Recovery then unfolds.

Toxic Shame Retards Awakening

If we had a "shame-o-meter" to measure effects one could, in all probability, observe an inverse relationship between shame and acceleration in recovery. The rate of acceleration or "Speed-Up" for AA occurred between 1935 and 1985 as public figures accepted the treatment. Exposed to broad public awareness, our social stigmas attached to alcoholism dissipated with participants and the general public. There are two factors to consider. First, is the inherent knowledge – shared by group members – of certainty of recovery for those choosing a commitment to change their minds. Next is the expansion of this "knowing" into broad public perspective. It was the coming together of a "critical few" that initiates the rapid change and acceleration. This creates a vital core of believers sufficient to transfer knowledge into a broader public awareness.

Where was the tipping point? We do not know the number of individuals that constitutes a critical mass in consciousness to quickened change of a spiritual nature. "*ACIM*" suggests it takes only two to effectively issue a "prayer of the heart." When two join together for a holy purpose, time collapses. As examples of the acceleration principle or "Speed-Up" in application, treatments for polio and alcoholism are like incubators. They show us "another way" to see how an individual's decision to change their mind about a concept can spread from one to many, and how the rate can accelerate rapidly when critical mass is obtained.

These are but two examples of human suffering. Wars, hunger, poverty and disease still dominate the human condition. Surely at least two or more will join and agree on these conditions' removal. All are called ... few choose to listen.

Seeing Beyond the Obstacles of Fear

The "*Course*'s" Voice asked Helen and Bill to accept their positions in this "present Speed-Up." Their assignment was to scribe "*A Course in Miracles*." They received a process to eradicate our paralyzing fear of the love of God residing in our minds. This is a process of individuation or awakening to the Christ-Self within. We are addicted to this fear; it keeps our egos in constant terror, hatred and confusion. It separates us from experiencing God's peace. Shame and guilt levels associated with addiction to this fear of awakening are intense. No wonder we refuse to look.

What Dr. Salk, Bill Wilson and Dr. Bob Smith had in common with Dr. Helen Schucman and Dr. Bill Thetford was the "little willingness" to see conditions differently. They shared a willingness to listen to this "call for love." Each responded to an inner voice or an inner awareness setting them on a path of discovery. Results were phenomenal as rates of change accelerated into our collective minds. Each of their biographies confirms how they struggled with this calling, resisting acceptance until all other paths disappeared. The "*Course*" will suggest our path is inevitable, and only time is optional. Fortunately, time is under our control.

Changing our mind is a reference to an option we have at any point "in time." We can choose to listen to the Voice for God or we can listen to our smaller self, our ego's voice. The ego only appears to speak first, because it speaks loudest. The very best choice our egos can produce is hatred. At any place in time, we are at a point of decision. The ego is that part of our mind which believes it is separated from our identity as the greater or Christ-Self. "*ACIM*" will refer to the domain of the ego as the wrong mind. God's Voice, the Spiritual Eye, is in our right mind. We are at a point of choice at every point "in time." We can choose whom we will listen to. Our Elder Brother has access to both spheres of our mind and is ever ready, listening for the miracle-minded. He will assist those who are ready to assume their place in the restoration program, The Plan of Atonement. He stands between us and Heaven and is ever listening for those miracle-minded, and equally ready to reach down and pull us up.

Our minds have a built-in capacity to choose for us. They need only a small amount of willingness to initiate change. Remember, our "little willingness" is really a decision to stop denying our unwillingness. In reality, we don't want the peace of God. Happiness is not our first choice. Our built-in facility's purpose is to choose for us. When we ask this facility to choose for us, it makes the decision to listen to the Voice for God, in our right mind. This is the Spiritual Eye's function.

The Spiritual Eye sees beyond our ego minds' fear, directing us to an experience of peace. It will re-present each situation from the perspective of a loving Father who wants the very best for his children. It offers an awareness surpassing anything we can comprehend with our ego minds. That is the Spiritual Eye's function, to choose for God for us. Anything beyond offering our "little willingness" will only hamper the re-presenting that results in peace of mind. It will only delay us "in time."

Offering our "little willingness" to the Spiritual Eye joins us with the goal of truth, God's general plan of transformation. We are given spiritual vision when we ask. We see beyond obstacles populating our ego mind. These restrict the flow of God's love. This request, or act, is the end to the beginning of terror. It is the beginning of the end of living in fear. Offering our "little willingness" is an acknowledgment we have accepted our place in God's Plan of At-One-Ment. This is our part a restoration plan.

Hearing from the Right Mind

As noted earlier, *"ACIM's"* first four chapters in the Hugh Lynn Cayce edition have concepts and terms that may differ from the most recently published Text. These chapters, as dictated to Helen and Bill, are metaphysical in nature. *"ACIM's"* remaining chapters were dictated using more traditional terms associated with Western Christianity.

For those with a predisposition to traditional and fundamental Christianity, it may take more time to remove blocks to the message. My personal introduction to *"A Course in Miracles"* followed a circuitous route. I was biased against traditional Christian terms. Concepts associated with the Holy Spirit, Jesus, spiritual healing and miracles were quite uncomfortable. For the several years, reading the published Text in our small group was a struggle. I was reluctant to embrace these Christian names. However, in time, I brought my incorrect beliefs to the internal Teacher, asking to see them differently. What evolved was an awareness of the universal concepts behind and beyond Christian names and symbols. Teachers appeared.

My prejudices toward "Holy Spirit," "Jesus," "spiritual healing" and "miracles" were obstacles to peace of mind. Rather than engage the spiritual Teacher in my mind, I chose resistance. I blamed traditional Christianity for their inerrant meanings, but I was the one who assigned definitions. It was my method of avoiding any sense of peace and happiness that was searching to find me. Reading the unedited version (the first four chapters of the Hugh Lynn Cayce version), I experienced less resistance to understanding a message of peace. Traditional Christian terms were no longer a barrier to knowledge. Words became symbols of symbols. No longer having insurmountable blocks to recovery, I began to see my prejudices that enabled my addiction to the fear of God.

For those who are predisposed to the same traditional Christian terminology as I was, you have a reprieve from agony. Becoming conscious of symbols of symbols – which the words represent, would have reduced the hesitation over terms and concepts that confused my mind. This is a significant personal "Speed-Up" in and of its own. Given time, I saw beyond these traditional meanings my ego assigned to Christian symbols. As the resistance lessened, I could hear the "*Course*'s" message.

I was confirmed into the Episcopal Church a number of years ago. I found the ritual of the Eucharist most reaffirming in understanding the Christian Holy Trinity. Mental concepts transformed, from theory to experiences, then a living reality. This was the result of listening to the right mind, or the Voice for God. This was how my vision was corrected by the Spiritual Eye, now individualized for my personal "unlearning experience." My ego thought system chose pain and torment. I could not blame my chosen misery on something Christian or external. These were my decisions to listen to the wrong voice in my mind.

The Course likens our resistance to participate in this "Speed-Up" to a baby that screams in rage at an adult taking away from him a knife or a pair of scissors. Such is our internal conflict on choosing. Reading the Text in a study group lessens the fear of looking at choices we have made. The shame and fear associated with these choices prohibit our awakening. We are given options to see these differently in a light that is neither fearful nor as terrorizing. This choice is available at any point "in time." The only precedent is offering a "little willingness."

Get Thee behind Me, Satan

One significant difference between the theology of "*ACIM*" and modern Christianity is the concept of taking error to truth, not the reverse. If the devil is a metaphor for the ego thought system in our own mind, going to the rooftop or mountaintop is the act of taking our wrong thinking to a higher place of learning in our right mind. This is what Jesus did; he took error to truth for correction. The parable's message could be get thee behind me Satan (ego or small self), or let me choose with the Voice for God, the Spiritual Eye.

Hideous experiences with those we despise, when given to the Spiritual Eye, will be seen in a new light. That is the Spiritual Eye's function: to see differently the imaginations of our own minds. As we give these aberrations up for correction, they become our greatest learning experiences. This traditional concept of the devil, in our mind, is one such misperception. The devil is in my thinking. I project it outward onto others, blaming someone else for my fear. Fortunately, evil is not out there, it's a thought in my mind.

Rather than devils as evil incarnate, our appointed enemies now become our teachers. They accelerate our awakening as we offer internal images for correction; now my attacker becomes my Savior. We only need offer a "little willingness" to see him differently – and our "little willingness" is really our awareness of the denial that we are unwilling. We refuse to acknowledge the unwillingness to let go of this decision to see another as a protagonist. We must be aware of the gravity in choosing with the ego thought system. Our decision to refuse the love of God is terrorizing; we cannot look alone.

The Voice of This Course

Discussing and sharing experiences in a group setting lessens our burden of fear. It facilitates a gentle awakening to truth, "in time." This is necessary in unlearning the ego thought system. The Text includes references to light as spiritual reality, or the Great Rays. Like the Spiritual Eye, this is an ancient symbol of the ultimate love of God. These predate Christianity as well. They are found in Egyptian mythology, modern Masonry and many religions. Our internal teacher's function is to remove obstructions blocking this light. "Standing in the Great Rays" can be understood as a symbol of experiencing God's unending love, now seen in light. Light becomes a symbol for our awakening to the Christ-Self, the Divine spirit within.

Before looking at the Book of Revelation, consider this re-presenting of a Biblical text as corrected by "ACIM's" Voice. You are familiar with this verse,

"Come unto me all ye that are weary and heavy laden, I will give you rest, for my yoke is easy and my burden light."

New meaning given by the Voice would instruct us to remember that "yoke" means "join together," and "burden" means "message." He asks us to reconsider the phrase:

"My yoke is easy and my burden light", in this wise;

"Let us join together, for my message is Light!"

Deceptions of Time and Speed

Speed and acceleration are measured in time, both deceptive in appearance. Shanghai's new super-speed Maglev train in the Peoples

Republic of China accelerates to 430 km/h. It was the world's fastest when installed. The 18-mile track has no conventional rails, the train no wheels. It zooms above guide rails on magnetic fields, taking eight minutes to go the same distance that could take hours in Shanghai traffic.

Gliding at 267 mph, one cannot detect the acceleration until an oncoming train passes at the same rate. The passing train does not appear as four cars. Instead, a six-inch wide black vertical line disappears in an instant. We know, in our mind, the train was much longer. When these two trains passed at accelerated speed, the illusion of a narrow black line is all that was visible. Our eyes can deceive us.

The Holy Instant

Our self-created fears are obstacles which protect us from experiencing God's love. When asked The Course's Voice and the Spiritual Eye's wisdom will flow over and around our obstacles as if they did not exist – when asked. The rate of flow is dependent upon our willingness to accept the gifts we seek. Forgiveness and peace of mind can appear as a slow coal train extending many miles in our vision, or just a thin black line flashing by in an instant. We call the latter a "Holy Instant." In this instant, our world and those who occupy it are transformed. This transformation takes place in our minds and appears as changes in the outer. These are perceptions corrected. This is the miracle.

Such can be our experience with apocalyptic fears imprisoning our mind with wars, hunger, poverty and disease. We can hold these thoughts for a thousand years while we endure endless Armageddons in agony and tribulation, or we can speed past these fears in the "twinkling of an eye." Terror is of our own making, not Heaven's reality. The choice is in our minds. Time and speed are under our control. This is the basis of a "Speed-Up." It must be used to our advantage. We need proper direction; we carry a heavy load. Fortunately, we know of another Voice and another way to look at time. It requires only a "little willingness."

Unload your burden! Our journey "in time" and "in reality," began long ago. Unlearning will quicken as we glide above and around fear at higher rates of acceleration. Taking our part in this "Celestial

Speed-Up" gives new meaning to time. Awakening to this message saves thousands of years "in time." As unlearning begins, we experience the "peace of mind" already in Heaven. We will feel the warmth of God's unending love as it surrounds us with Great Rays of hope. As minds join together to unlearn, they awaken. Thousands of others will also experience this Love of God, pouring unabated through the portal we will create as a "Circle of Forgiveness."

What follows in the next few chapters is a re-presenting of the Book of Revelation and a further explanation of *A Course in Miracles'* concepts. It can be used as a personal guide to organize and facilitate study groups. For those who choose to function as teachers, this will set them on their way. This requires us to join hands with our fellows and offer the "little willingness" to look beyond our reservoirs of fear and shame. We are near the tipping point for acceleration. What appears on our mental horizon is a promised land of happiness. This is our New Jerusalem, as promised in the "End Times" myths.

It is time to reconsider false meanings given to our Myths of the Apocalypse and End Times. They cloud our memory and maintain a tiny gap separating us from our own Divinity. They are no longer needed. Together, we can choose "another way" to look at these misperceptions. Together, we accelerate, "in time," on our path to Heaven -- because time, as we know it, is coming to an end.

Chapter 4

Revelation and the Last Judgment

"Prepare you NOW for the undoing of what never was..."

The Happy Dream, "ACIM"

Revelation is an integral part of the Judeo-Christian message. It has endless meanings depending on the branch and sect of our lineage. We need to discuss the revelations of John, the Book of Revelation's author and known by most scholars as John of Patmos. He received his revelations in a cave on the Island of Patmos. These are the source of our obsession with "End Times." Revelation, as used in *"A Course in Miracles,"* is intended to describe the highest means of communication with our Creator. It descends from Heaven to us, not in the other direction. Many Western religions employ this similar concept of revelation. The problem begins with the revelation given to John of Patmos.

We don't know whether John was a disciple, political organizer, a contemporary of Jesus or just another troubled soul. We do know his revelations have wreaked havoc on every generation since putting pen to parchment. What if John's revelations were intended for his eyes only, and not the rest of the world? One means of judging a spiritual truth's validity is by the fruit it bears. "Ultimate Spiritual Knowledge" or "Revelation," as defined by *"ACIM,"* has only one consequence: peace of mind. If peace does not ensue, there was no Revelation. Knowledge reveals itself in many ways. Our minds project truth onto physical forms we understand. Teachers are such forms. They reflect our message of truth, bringing it into conscious awareness. Our internal voice for truth is faint. Eventually it resonates, but at first it is still and silent. We need each other to hear our internal voices and to learn. In this way, learning is reflected through our brother's mind; now amplified, it is unavoidable. I speak of our brothers as all mankind, in both the collective and fraternal sense; both become our teachers. This is a divine plan. This is the process of forgiveness.

There is value in group study. When two or more come together for the expressed purpose of experiencing truth, miraculous things happen. Casual encounters now take on holy purposes. This is the plan of forgiveness in practice. It expresses itself in forms of unlearning. The ego thought system hypnotizes our minds with messages of self hatred and destruction. So vile are these messages, we refuse to look upon their untruth for fear of perishing. Instead, we project it onto our brothers. Individually, this message maintains conflict and discord. Collectively, it creates terror, wars and chaos. We must learn to recognize our projections. This is the function of our voice for truth. It is in all minds. Every thought of discord also has a holy purpose. When given to the "voice for truth" in our mind, it is reinterpreted.

A message of truth establishes peace of mind. Any thought other than truth does not. This becomes a touchstone for all thoughts. Learning to apply this measure is the process of willingness. "A Course in Miracles" asks this simple question:

"Does this thought I hold produce peace of mind?"

Expressed in another way, do I like the way I feel? Learning to ask this question is monumental. Becoming willing to hear its response will relieve self-damnation. Responding to the answer will save us all from self-destruction.

Looking at deeply held beliefs that produce terror requires help. We cannot do this alone. When walking the edge of a crevice, it is best to hold a hand, lest we slip. The Book of Revelation and the Apocalyptic Myth are such beliefs. Nothing will produce fear and the ensuing chaos like these tales of woe. If peace is the measure of truth, these myths do not produce peace of mind. Better stated, our interpretation does not produce peace of mind. When given to the "voice for truth," a different message appears. Our fear resides and another message appears.

Dispensationalist, Russia and Y2K

The motivation for these words came from viewing "Left Behind," a popular movie from the novel of the same name. This is the first in a series of dramatic depictions rendering a traditional and literal understanding of "End Times" philosophy. These events are chosen from the Book of Revelation, The Book of Daniel and writings of St. Paul, with a strong dose of fatalism and dispensationalism.

Dispensationalists believe in a theological system that breaks history into specific periods. It was developed in the mid-19th century by an English theologian, John Nelson Darby, and perhaps most significantly, it integrates excerpts from both the Old and New Testaments supporting a doomsday scenario of death and destruction. The theory was popularized in the early 1900s with publication of "*Scofield's Reference Bible.*" This work cross-referenced Biblical quotations, allowing readers to follow from book to book and chapter to chapter. Here are excerpts from Scofield's notes on the Battle of Armageddon, which *concludes* Russia will lead the attack against Israel:

"That the primary reference is to the northern (European) powers, headed up by Russia, all agree. The whole passage should be read in connection with Zechariah 12:1-4 and 14:1-9; Matthew 24:14-30; and Revelation 14:14-20 and 19:17-21. "Gog" is the prince, "Magog," his land. The reference to Meshach and Tubal (Moscow and Tools) is a clear mark of identification. Russia and the northern powers have been the latest persecutors of dispersed Israel, and it is congruous both with divine justice and with the covenants (e.g. Genesis 15:18). Deuteronomy 30:3 says destruction should fall at the climax of the last mad attempt to exterminate the remnant of Israel in Jerusalem. The whole prophecy belongs to the yet future "day of Jehovah" (Isaiah 2:10-22 and Revelation 19:11-21) and to the battle of Armageddon (Revelation 16:14 Also see "Revelation 19:19" but includes also the final revolt of the nations at the close of the kingdom-age (Revelation 20:7-9).

As you can see, Scofield has stitched together a string of references to support his conclusion: Russia will attack Israel. You may wish to read these excerpts and determine if you find the same results. Words are but symbols of symbols; they reflect information in our own minds. We decide with either our egos or the Voice for God, and then send out messengers to find evidence supporting our decisions. The measure of truth is the product of our decision; does it produce peace of mind?

We are again obsessed with Middle Eastern wars and must ask, are these fulfillments of Scofield's prophecy? If not, have we remade a decision with the ego for destruction and now send forth messengers to affirm our accord? Irrespective of the cause, this is a message of inevitable conflict with perceived good fighting evil; it is an unconscious myth as old as time. Unfortunately, when it reappears in our conscious mind, through the ages, each side takes up arms and names the evil ones for battle. For 20th Century Americans, the mold has been cast. The Book of Revelation, with support from other chapters of the Bible, has prescribed a cocktail of chaos. We continue to add toxic ingredients. With this concoction in hand, evangelical ministers in the late 1800's spread a tale of horrific destruction to congregations starved for entertainment. The modern fundamentalist movements evolved from this type of reasoning, and continue to dispense fear baiting-sermons today. They reflect a purposeful sampling of theology rather than discerning study. It serves our ego minds well; confusion and fear always follow. This must be our measure of truth.

My first reaction was to discount the *"Left Behind"* series as fiction. No one could believe the stories are literal. Then I remembered our response to the Y2K fiasco. Visiting old high school friends in Southern Missouri, I was appalled with the many who had bought power generators and stockpiled water, fuel and food. They were convinced the world was ending at 12:01 am in the year 2000. These were beliefs espoused by area ministers who were products of local bible colleges, mostly prophets of doom and literalism. The colleges' fundamentalist theologies were inspired by the teachings of Darby, Scofield and others, whose evangelical zeal spread west during the turn of the last century. These Dispensationalists were alive in my mind as well, now projected onto my contemporaries. Y2K affected every major corporation in the United States. Imagine the power this Myth maintains in our mind, forcing us to spend billions on reprogramming for an event that did not happen.

Hillel Schwartz' *"Century's End"* is an excellent account of society's reaction to the passing of previous centuries and the last millennium. His writing details how Europe responded to 1000 AD with fear and reactions not dissimilar to those in 2000 AD. Commerce stopped, waiting on the end. It took years to regenerate – a reoccurring theme in our minds. Hidden under layers of denial, this saga reappears at first opportunity, striking terror in every heart. According to Schwartz' account, it was decades before any social and economic recovery followed the standstill. This was the enlightened world awaiting destruction at 12:01 a.m. in 1000, "in time." The Great Crusades began in earnest around 1095 and continued until 1291. European Christians were called to the Holy Lands to defeat the evil hordes occupying Jerusalem. History doesn't repeat itself, but it does rhyme.

Another Way

Paralyzed with fear, I decided to apply my own measure of truth. I asked if there was "another way" to see this Apocalyptic Myth of terror that was being projected onto my friends, movies and literature. There must be another way, I thought. Mindful of my fear, I began to research terms and concepts traditionally associated with "End Times" philosophies from "*A Course in Miracles.*" More specifically, I looked for those supporting an eminent eschatology or immediate end to this world. Using my word processor's search engine, I scoured the unpublished edition of "*A Course in Miracles.*" Then, I read the published edition of the "*Workbook*" and "*Manual for Teachers,*" looking for terms used in the Apocalyptic Myth. I was seeking definitions by "*ACIM*'s" Author. The answers did not come in a neat package in one section. Instead, the same message was repeated over and over throughout the entire Text. It appeared as new meanings for core terms used in the Apocalyptic Myth and from a section in the teacher's manual, "*How Will Time End?*".

Relevant terms appeared with clear and refreshing words of hope. "*ACIM*" does not support a Doomsday scenario resulting in the world's destruction. Rather, it suggests terms such as Revelation and rapture which, `discerned spiritually, are intended to awaken our Divinity. Nothing in the Text suggests a divine plan of tribulation or chaos, other than what we choose collectively with our own ego minds. Since it is of our own making, we can choose again at any time. The Apocalyptic Myth is in our mind, not God's. We only need to be willing to see it another way, and then ask our internal Teacher for help.

I facilitated our local Miracles study group the next Sunday. My lesson plan included references from "*ACIM,*" with definitions as a handout for reading and discussion. Fortunately, my classmates were accomplished students. Most were well-versed in "*ACIM*'s" origins and content, having previously read the Course. One delightful couple had dinner with Dr. Bill Thetford, who compiled the original dictation with Dr. Helen Schuman Several had studied with Dr. Kenneth Wapnick, who edited the Text's published version. And some were students of

Edgar Cayce, having known Hugh Lynn Cayce. They had studied a copy of the Course before its publication. We also had many visitors that day who were well-informed students, all of which created an atmosphere electric with curiosity. These were the modern-day scribes and Pharisees of "*A Course in Miracles.*"

A New Revelation

My challenge to the class: there must be "another way" to look at the Book of Revelation, the Apocalypse and The End of Time. With my handout, we read each section or paragraph that dealt with concepts and terms normally assigned to Revelation, the Apocalypse and End Time scenarios.

What unfolded was a hectic, energetic exchange of research, discussion and knowledge. The results were astounding. I was challenged to absorb this stream of understanding, which concluded in a most reassuring message. What emerged was an entirely new way of looking at the Apocalypse's fear-based concepts and the end of time. We reached a conclusion far different than Scofield's . The allegory became a story about awakening our internal spiritual Self, not a diatribe about external events. Our fear of awakening to our Christ-Self had been denied, then projected outward as these horrific "End Times" prophecies.

These definitions will be reviewed in the following chapters. They need not be accepted, but they do need to be acknowledged. To initiate the process of unlearning, it is important to read what is being presented. In time, they can be revisited. An internal Teacher is always available, and will determine if this message is true for each of us. This is the Elder Brother residing in our right minds. He knows Heaven's reality. The measure of truth is peace of mind, which always follows. The miracle is a change in perception. Our special relationship with the "Archetype of the Apocalypse" is changing into a holy relationship. Our fear will lead to the conscious awakening of the Divine Christ in everyone.

We must join in this unlearning experience. It is incumbent upon each of us to offer our "little willingness." We only need look at our unwillingness to acknowledge our denial of these fear-based concepts. This is preventing us from experiencing peace of mind. We need do nothing else. Ask your internal Teacher to see them differently. Doing this as a group makes it a shared experience and accelerates the awakening of a corrected message. Uncommon knowledge will become common knowledge. In reality, these apocalyptic nightmares were never true; they were just an unlearning experience awaiting our internal Teacher's proper use. I was amazed at the transformational experience when I become willing to see them differently. The process begins when one is willing to hear another new voice. Fear will evaporate; the remaining void will be instantly filled with a loving truth we can easily understand. True Revelation is at hand.

"Prepare you now for the undoing of what never was." "ACIM"

The Other Way

"ACIM's" author defines Revelation as an experience inspired directly by God. Judeo-Christian and Islamic religions all use the term as a means of describing direct communication with God. Revelation is not exclusive to the concepts or prophecies outlined in the Book of Revelation, yet it has a strong correlation in Western minds.

The following are all true statements about Revelation, as defined by *"ACIM"*:

- *It induces complete but temporary suspension of doubt and fear.*
- *It represents the original form of communication between God and His Souls or Children.*
- *It involves an extremely personal sense of closeness to Creation.*
- *Revelation unites Souls directly with God.*

As a metaphor for personal awakening or individuation, Revelation is another name for a spiritual break-through. This is one stage of awakening where the lesser or ego-self becomes conscious of the higher Christ-Self. This is our awareness going beyond any intellectual concept. It now centers at the experiential level. We are like Job, overwhelmed with doubt and self-condemnation, as he becomes conscious of his new concept of Yahweh, or Jesus on the Mount of Transfiguration, with disciples who now see Him with new eyes. Revelation is another name for breakthrough; it is the "peak or oceanic" experiences referenced earlier. These experiences transpire outside of "time."

Revelation brings forth a state in which fear has already been abolished, is intensely personal and cannot actually be translated into conscious content at all. Any attempt to describe Revelation in words is usually incomprehensible. Revelation induces only experience. It is personal to the receiver. Revelation is the universal experience. It is not only possible, but necessary. Edinger put it in these words:

"In psychological terms, it is a revelation of the archetypal psyche which releases one from a personal ego-attitude, enabling one to experience oneself as an immortal--that is, as living with archetypal realities and making a contribution to the archetypal psyche."(Citing Frey) "Death is for me the gate to a new birth, and the breaking-through of the transcendental realm into our empirical existence. I am convinced that we experience a complete transformation of our being in the last moments of our life."

(Edward Edinger, MD, "Anatomy of the Psyche" p128)

The Book of Revelation from Christianity's New Testament is based on a series of dreams revealed to John of Patmos around 90 A.D. Most scholars agree he was not John the Baptist or John the Apostle. It is significant that his revelations were in dream format. John's dreams were transmitted by letters to early Christians in Asia Minor. Some believe John's purpose was to dissuade his readers from participating in pagan rituals of local trade unions. These letters have been the subject of speculation, fear and terror since they were written.

The visions were received in a cave. Spiritual messages or epistles given to enlighten usually come from mountaintop experiences. The Sermon on the Mount, the Ten Commandments and the Transfiguration all took place on a mountain peak. As a symbol, one can understand the mountain as a high point or place of learning in our minds, the Self or Christ mind. Those receiving these messages were able to rise in consciousness, having direct communication with God. This is the process of turning illusion into truth. These experiences were transformational to giver and receivers. These Revelations were received from God, but not as dreams.

Did John of Patmos receive a true revelation, or did he receive a veiled message that would lead us out of the dark cavern of denial and fear, where we hide from our true spiritual identity? St. Ignatius Loyola's breakthrough experience was in a cave, but his message of individual awakening came later. Jonas in the belly of the whale did not receive an epistle; he finally broke his denial. The questions must be asked, does the experience of John of Patmos' message produce peace of mind? If so, then is it a true Revelation as defined by "*ACIM*?"

One could suggest that John of Patmos was experiencing archetypal energies speaking directly to him about his own individuation. We know of him only by his dreams, not by any other ministries or missions he may have conducted. Why are his visions and dreams considered so significant? They have not produced peace of mind, but instead have had a horrific effect on our global consciousness as "End Times" prophecies.

Perhaps symbolically, John of Patmos is leading us out of a dark, dank place in our minds ...our cave of self-loathing and hatred. Here we entombed our most precious gift, the Christ-Self. In some perverse way, our ego-self tells us we have crucified our Christ-Self and must be punished. We do this with a horrific tale of doomsday scenarios, with "end of time" dates continually reset to extend the terror in our minds. Seeing a light of truth, our mountain top experience appears. We must remove the dark veil that blinds us to the Spirit. Until the fallacies of Armageddon and End Times are exposed to the light of day, we cannot see lessons of the Spirit. Until our errant belief in a literal Apocalypse is unveiled, we cower in darkness. We cannot stand in a light of forgiveness.

Lifting the Veil

Apocalypse is the Greek term for revelation, meaning literally to pull away the covers or veil. John of Patmos' dreams are a description of the chaos and horror promised by our ego minds. Any chaotic "End Times' " myth is only a threat. It foretells the wrath to unfold should we begin to reconsider our decision. This decision is the treaty made with our wrong mind, the ego-self's home and basis for false beliefs. We have not been separated from our Christ-Self; we have only veiled our decision in a belief of separation. This is the unholy union we have made with our ego minds and have promised never to look upon again.

Martin Luther gave no credibility to the Book of Revelation. He suggested these visions were neither prophetic nor apostolic. Jesus taught us to love our neighbor, heal the sick, feed the hungry and visit those in prison. Yet we still cling to this tale like rats to driftwood, abandoned on the sea. We choose terror when love is offered.

"*A Course in Miracles*" presents The Book of Revelation's concepts as having little to do with our Apocalyptic Myth's traditional beliefs or "End Times' "concepts. The only relationship is Revelation, as defined by "*ACIM,*" completely abolishes our belief in separation from the Christ-Self by removing our fear of God. This is the precursor to the "End of Time." Our greatest terror is releasing the fear of God. This is the decision we have made and upon which we have taken a vow never to revisit. This is a pact with our ego minds, the devil in our thinking. We have projected it outward for so long and so far, it has dissociated in our minds.

To understand the magnitude of this fear is to imagine our world's complete and total destruction. Our ultimate nightmare is tremendous suffering. It smolders like an ember covered by ashes, smugly concealed under layers of denial in our unconscious minds. So great is this denial's energy that when ignited, it flashes outward and destroys unsuspecting targets. These are children abandoned in preemptive wars, the starving, and the downtrodden who wander streets of desolate cities seeking shelter from our storms. This is the real Apocalypse: the rotten fruit of our modern-day misunderstandings of revelation. It is happening now; we need not wait for a future date. Terror's choice is in our minds. Atrocities are of our own making, not God's.

Look upon the faces of horror. Like a mirror they will reflect the denial in our own minds. This is the face of pain and suffering presented to us for redemption. Ask your internal Teacher, the Christ within, to see beyond these faces of terror. We will be able to cast our eyes upon Christ's face. We will see salvation as it reaches outward to offer forgiveness. Answering this call for love will bridge our minds' gap of denial.

By offering healing to the least of us, we accept healing for ourselves. This is God's Plan of Atonement. This is what we shroud in an apocalyptic myth – the reflection of Christ within ourselves. This is the Love of God flowing through us, bringing spiritual healing to both sender and receiver. We will understand true Revelation has a much greater purpose than presenting a tale of destruction. Its messages include healing the sick, feeding the hungry and visiting the imprisoned. We are sick from our fear, we hunger for spiritual renewal and we are imprisoned by this tale of death and destruction. We seek another way.

"*ACIM*'s Author– the internal Voice and Teacher – indirectly inspires Revelation. His function is to remain alert to our readiness. Revelation comes directly from God to our minds, as it was with John of Patmos. We must apply "*ACIM*'s" measure of instruction; Revelation is extremely personal and cannot be translated into someone else's conscious content. Any attempt to express John's experience in written form would be incomprehensible. (We should say it is incomprehensible.) Do John's dreams, which became the Book of Revelation, produce peace in the world, or even peace of mind? The answer is obvious: no.

Your Worst Nightmare

Assume you had such a dream. Upon awakening, you jotted down the nightmare's recollections in a diary, understanding them only as dreams, and not reality. Many years later, someone finds your diary and decides it has significant meaning. Your notes are published with countless interpretations having no bearing on your experience. This lurid dream takes a life of its own, with no relationship to your understanding. What results are wars, famines, pestilence and never-ending conflict. This must be the way John of Patmos would have felt. Such a beautiful personal experience, but so misunderstood.

This is a significant point. Countless interpretations have been given to the Book of Revelation. Revelation is always individual, as defined by "*ACIM*." Its true understanding is for the one receiving the message. Taking someone's experience of Revelation is like trying to share intimacy between you and your partner with someone else; it never makes the translation. What if John of Patmos' dreams were really about his personal experiences of awakening from the depths of fear? Using our "*ACIM*" definition, Revelation involves an extremely personal sense of closeness to Creation. We try to replicate this spiritual intimacy in physical relationships. Unfortunately, physical closeness cannot achieve the same level of intimacy we seek with our mind Christ-Self. We are always left wanting: more food, more pleasure.

Our centuries of grief, guilt and anxiety over human interpretations of the Book of Revelation are works of our ego minds. This is our physical eye, or in Christian terms, the Devil. You may validate this hypothesis with its results. Fear, anxiety and hostile interaction are not motivated by true Revelation. Jesus of Nazareth quoted scriptures to resist the Devil's temptations (or in this context, the voice of the ego). He chose to hear "another way," prompting Him to seek truth. Jesus listened to another voice. When fear of Revelation rises, we must say, *"Get thee behind me Satan. You have no power over me lest it came from God above."* We must do no less.

Even more important is our assurance God will reveal Himself to each of us. That is a promise from the *"Course's"* Voice, who is always listening and seeking those who are revelation-ready. When we individually are prepared for Revelation, this internal voice for truth will induce transmission. Some equate the internal voice with *"ACIM's"* author. Sometimes, it is referred to as our Elder Brother. Irrespective of the name, it is the part of our mind responsible for teaching the truth. This is knowledge from the Spiritual Eye, the communication link with God. As individuals, we all have this ability. Fear is abolished when we listen to the Voice for God. Peace always ensues. Joy and happiness will lead down this path.

Those who experience Revelation will know; they don't need to tell or to be told. We will understand through the awareness of our knowledge. This is the smile on a face and the presence of peace that we will want to experience. Some may remember this verse from a Christian hymn, *"And they will know we are Christians by our love, by our love. They will know we are Christians by our love."* A Book of true Revelation can produce only peace of mind.

The Last Judgment

Next to the fear of God's love, the Last Judgment is mankind's greatest threat. "Judging" thoughts engender our tremendous fear of God. These images of divine yet capricious verdicts have been rendered by us, not God. Fear exists because of our false beliefs of being separated from God. This is the definition of sin. Believing we could live outside of Heaven's peace and contentment is our original sin. Indeed, it is our only sin. Abolishing this belief is the precursor to the End of Time.

Just as our myth of separation from God started many millions of years ago, the Last Judgment may extend over a similarly long period of time. The length of the Last Judgment depends on the effectiveness of this present "Speed-Up." "ACIM's" Voice tells us this. He also tells us the love of God is His only creation. As the Sonship, we are pure love, His complete and perfect creations. The Sonship is that part of our right mind we share with God and each other. This is our Divinity within. It is also the memory of God's love in each of our minds. Jesus of Nazareth is one who completely embodied this love. It was a memory that became a practical experience. Anything other than God's love is of our own making."ACIM" distinguishes between creating and making; only God can create. This distinction between God's creations and what we have made is significant in understanding correction.

Creating versus Making

We can extend God's love -- which is the miracle – but we cannot create by and of ourselves. When we call upon the voice of the truth and the Spiritual Eye to decide for us, we are co-creating with God. This is our highest function. We "make" when we decide with our egos and project these decisions onto our brothers. This results in mis-creations. What we have made in our minds and projected into our world is truncated. It boggles our imagination and will not rectify the ego mind. Further, we are in denial of this decision. This is a treaty "made" with our ego. We vow never to look at its origins. This is the source of our "unwillingness."

The Last Judgment could be called a process of right evaluation. It means as we come to understand all those things we have "made," it will become obvious which are worthy and which aren't. As we choose to hear the voice for God or see with the Spiritual Eye, our ability to choose can be reasonably directed. We will vacillate between freedom and imprisonment until we learn to discern between God's creations and those things we have made with our egos. Our first step toward freedom entails sorting the true and false.

This sorting-out process is the act of dividing our minds' righteous thoughts from the unrighteous, but only in the constructive sense. This reflects the Apocalypse's true meaning Remember, apocalypse means to "lift the veil." Our ego minds have used upside-down thinking by taking a term intended to mean awakening, and given it the opposite meaning. I will explain "upside-down thinking" further along, but suffice to say these are the false beliefs we assign to disturbing terms and concepts to protect ourselves from God's love. Upside-down thinking is a means our smaller or ego-self uses to reverse intent and hide its true meaning.

We can look at our fear of End Times in another way. The terror and chaos traditionally associated with apocalyptic thinking are resistance to looking at thoughts "made" in our own minds. Specifically, these are thoughts made with the ego minds, but attributed to God. We project these onto our fellow man. Collectively and individually, we must ultimately look upon these thoughts, which we have "made" separate and apart from God. We can decide to preserve only what is good. This is just as God himself looked upon what He had created and knew it was good. This is the final judgment we will make.

In reality, the Last Judgment is not a procedure God undertakes, but one for which each individual is responsible. We do it collectively for mankind. More specifically, each of us must hold the hand of the Course's voice, our internal Teacher, as we stand in judgment of ourselves. We determine what we have made with our ego, as opposed to what we have co-created with God.

The Last Judgment is a "final healing." This is not a righteous distribution of punishment or an ultimate day in court. A capricious god does not sort the chosen from those not chosen, the righteous and the unrighteous. Wheat and chaff, sheep and goats ... these are illusions in our minds. These decisions and thoughts we made will become our maximal learning experiences. These are opportunities for forgiveness.

Remember, all have been chosen; we only need listen to the Spiritual Eye. Hold the hand of the Course's Voice. It will give us ears to hear the "Voice for God." We respond to him as if he were an Elder Brother who has already undergone the process and knows the ropes. Justice will be dispensed when we make this decision to call on our personal teacher and listen to the Spiritual Eye. This is our day in court. The verdict we render will be innocent in the eyes of God. There are no other options.

The Last Judgment as Miracles in Time

Miracles are time-shortening devices. Revelation is experienced totally outside of time. As we extend the love of God to any of our fellows, we perform miracles. This initiates an "out-of-pattern" sequence in which we and our brothers experience forgiveness. We emerge further along "in time." Studying in group settings will clearly form in each person's mind the idea of miracles as a time-saving device.

For the purposes of this discussion, let's assume the effects of miracles can save thousands of years in time. Since time is a concept we have made within our egos, it exists only in our minds. Time expands to fill our needs. More than 1 million years ago, the earth's rotation was the equivalent of 18 hours a day. Even now, a day is not 24 hours long, but 23 hours plus. We have created standards for time. Only in the last 40 years have we standardized the length of a second.

Perhaps you are familiar with our global positioning system (GPS). Just as the advent of transcontinental railroads standardized time in the United States more than a century ago, so has GPS expanded our application in this century. Columbus discovered the world was not flat, but we have discovered it is not round, either. The earth's surface is an irregular shape; we use geoids in quadrants to derive standards for geo-positioning. Geoids are theoretical shapes we have made and will vary according to various mapping standards. As you can see, the entire global positioning system is based on theoretical shapes, in time. What we see on a map is only an image created by our mind, not the actual position of the surface. Yet, we consider this reality.

X Never Marks the Spot

"X," which marks the spot on your GPS in your car dashboard, is not the spot. It is just a theory of where "X" could be, based on transmissions from several GPS satellites. Unless you are with U.S. Armed Forces, the accuracy will vary from one to five meters horizontally. These positions are based on standardized time in milliseconds and the earth's rotational speed. From this data, we determine our place in space and time. Time has become so widely accepted these theoretical concepts became facts. Our fundamental belief in time has become literal and now, inerrant.

We also believe Heaven is separate in space and time. However, if our modern concepts of time are based on theoretical models we have made, the earth's rotational speed is variable (over time) and if the second is a consensus standard, which part of time is real? What is the distance between us and Heaven? Can we measure it in space or time? If the Bible is inerrant and factual, how real is the time and space that separates us from Heaven? We worship science and its methods, but they offer no answers to these questions.

A revelatory experience happens outside our concept of time. This awareness does not need time to register; it does not recognize time as real. Neither does God. Miracles create an out-of-pattern sequence, in time, which has the effect of saving time. We made time with our ego minds and believe it is real. The voice for God uses miracles to shorten time. It also narrows the distance we believe is separating us from the love of God in Heaven. When we offer miracles to our fellow man, we both emerge further along in time. This is how miracles save time. As a sufficient number of people become truly miracle-minded, the time-saving process will accelerate; time will be shortened almost immeasurably. The miracle shortens the distance we believe separates us from the Love of God, in space and time.

"ACIM" tells us our belief in separation from God and Heaven – the original sin – took place millions of years ago "in-time." The Last Judgment can take just as long. However, as more individuals free themselves from fear and heal personal conflicts, we all emerge further along in time. This change in mind, or our release of non-truth, has a cumulative effect in acceleration. As more of us question our concepts of time by offering forgiveness through the means of miracles, the rate of change will increase. The curve goes up steeply, creating critical mass. It will initiate a change in our thinking – like the polio vaccine – and it will come into broad public awareness. As fear and shame are reduced, love fills their void.

When each of us submits to the Last Judgment, we move closer to Heaven. Our belief in the original sin weakens. Coincidently, we will strengthen our beliefs in celestial and heavenly bodies as ideas of peace in our minds. What was an ancient melody becomes a present memory. The result will be the current "Celestial Speed-Up."

In reality, the true process of the Last Judgment takes place in our own minds as we begin to look – with love – on what we have made.

We can reconsider what we have made and determine its worthiness. The mind will inevitably disown its miscorrelations as we individually begin to look within. The choices will become obvious as we develop lines of communication with "*ACIM*'s" Voice.

The Last Judgment and Upside-Down Thinking

The Last Judgment is frightening because it has been falsely projected onto God. It is also frightening because of the association of "last" with death. The Text calls this "upside-down thinking." This is one way our ego-mind reverses concepts, keeping us in everlasting confusion. This is the hell we have made for ourselves. In this example, the process of judging should not be related with death. In reality, this is our doorway to life. Our ego mindset takes this concept and turns it upside down to keep us confused.

This is a crucial concept we must better understand. What follows is an important example demonstrating the relevance of "upside-down thinking." Learning to question our thoughts and listen to the voice for God is central to the process of removing obstacles to awakening.

In 1961, Dr. Carl Jung wrote a letter to Bill Wilson, a founder of Alcoholics Anonymous, responding to a request concerning a former Jung patient – and a friend of Wilson – in recovery. Wilson wanted to know about the disease of alcoholism and its obsession for drinking to the point of death.

Wilson's friend was an early AA member and instrumental in explaining a spiritual awakening is prerequisite to any sustained recovery from alcoholism. The friend had been treated by Jung in Switzerland before AA's founding in 1935. Jung told his patient that without a deep and effectual psychic change of mind, recovery was hopeless and death would follow. What Dr. Jung conveyed to Wilson's friend was equally startling; his alcoholism was not caused by moral deficiency, but was instead an unconscious obsession for the ultimate experience with the Divine within. It is a craving for a spiritual breakthrough.

Jung told Wilson his friend's alcoholic cravings were equivalent to the spiritual thirst of our "being." This is our soul's thirst for completeness, our wholeness with God. In medieval terms this was referred to as "Union with God." The only way to experience this

Union was to walk a narrow path that led to a higher state of understanding. One could be led by grace, through contacts with friends or through education in a "higher place of learning" in our mind. Jung was convinced the ego-thought system (devil or evil) led our unfulfilled and unrecognized need for "Union with the Spirit" into perdition. Someone without a pathway to follow or divine protection could not successfully make this journey. The pull of our ego-thought system was too great for a solo traveler to overcome.

Thirst for the Spirit

The Latin term 'spiritus" has dual meanings. Jung notes that spirit in the U.S. could mean a high level of religious or spiritual experience. It could also mean spirits, a depraving poison when consumed in excess. He concluded our confused ego mind mistook an insatiable craving for spiritual understanding and turned it "upside down." The craving for "Union with the Spirit" became a compulsion for drinking alcohol and a destructive obsession. His formula was: spiritus contra spiritum.

When observed by a discerning mind, our greatest poison became a pathway to our most prized experience. Jung ended his letter to Wilson from Psalm 42:

"As the deer panteth after the brook's water,

So panteth my soul after thee, O God.

My Soul thirsts for Thee."

Recovery from alcoholism is a specific application to correct upside-down thinking. Our ego mind takes what was intended as "thirst for the Spirit" and turns it upside down. It becomes a deadly compulsion to "thirst for" or consume alcoholic spirits.

Newcomers to AA cannot comprehend the magnitude of their cravings during early recovery. No attempt is made to persuade a trembling alcoholic his true obsession is for spiritual union with God. The trauma of alcohol withdrawal requires commencement at a simpler level, the narrower path Jung suggested. In time, the need for spiritual renewal becomes apparent, but the process involves unlearning old thought patterns. The awakening becomes a byproduct of the recovery steps, some gradual, but others more abrupt. What follows in recovery is an understanding at the spiritual-craving level, not just the physical level. Yet the awakening truly begins at a point much earlier with the decision to seek life, not death, through alcohol poisoning. This process unfolds in time, but is necessary for sustained recovery. This is the Spiritual Eye's proper use of time.

Upside-down thinking is cured through a gradual healing process, allowing a gentle awakening to the truth. This is the same promise suggested by "ACIM's" Voice. Just as an alcoholic cannot comprehend the real nature of craving during detoxification, we cannot bear the truth of our obsession with apocalyptic thinking. We will be slowly led to reality. Some experience awakening by reading the "ACIM's" text. Here the spiritual Teacher's presence emerges into our conscious understanding. A program of restoration is personalized for each of us to follow. This is the beginning to the end of our obsession with "end times" thinking.

The Apocalypse and Upside-Down Thinking

As previously mentioned, apocalypse in Greek means to pull back the cover or remove the veil. In this context, we are pulling back the veil of separation made to keep us apart from our spiritual identity and the peace of God. Our ego minds have taken experiences intended to signal our awakening to the spirit within and turned them upside down. This impulse for spiritual understanding has become our ultimate nightmare. We ask the ego to choose fear for us, when peace is offered.

The Peace of God has many meanings. In many Christian churches, parish members offer the Peace of God to each other following liturgical communion. One modern-day use stems from a 12th-Century Catholic Pope who declared the "Peace of God." He issued a proclamation prohibiting knights traveling to the Great Crusades' Holy Wars from killing peasants along the way. He thought this was needless slaughter. This is not the Peace of God we are seeking.

Here is a definition of fear from "ACIM," describing the absence of peace:

> *"You ARE fearful if you do not feel-*
>
> *A deep content*

A certainty of help

A calm assurance

Heaven goes with you,"

"ACIM"

The ego's voice speaks simultaneously with God's voice. The latter is much quieter, but it will always be heard when we choose to listen. The ego's voice only appears to speak first because it always speaks the loudest. When we chose to listen to the voice for God or see with the Spiritual Eye, our request is always answered. Our vision will be corrected and we proceed in our functions, effortlessly. That is the miracle: the natural profession of the Children of God

Our ego mind incorrectly takes the definition of these terms and uses them as obstacles to our awakening. Like the idea of time, they become strongly entrenched in our collective unconscious. However, our upside-down thinking can be corrected. Jung began the correction of our preconceptions on alcoholism. His suggestion of the need for a spiritual or religious experience to sustain recovery was shared with Wilson. Alcoholism became a pathway to spiritual awakening.

We must start the process of correcting misinterpretations about Last Judgment and the "End of Time." Jung's message of hope was carried to Wilson by an unbroken chain of events. It became a central theme of recovery in AA. Seeing AA's history of gradual public acceptance as a recovery program is important. Only a critical few were able to grasp the concept and bring it into early understanding and practice. The rapid spread in corrected perception, with an increasing rate in acceleration, is an application of a "Speed-Up."

It Is We Who Make the Last Judgment

"*ACIM*" suggest God's judgment cannot be directed toward us. This is a misperception. As God's creations and beings, we are complete with Him. He cannot and does not judge us. We will also correct our misperception about time. The only purpose of time is to "give us time" to separate thoughts we have made with our egos from those thoughts that are co-creations with God.

93

Our instruction is to retain only those thoughts that are extensions of God's Love. "*ACIM*" defines this as right-mindedness. This choosing or separation of thoughts must be made in a metaphorical sense. Living in fear of God is really not being alive. Do only this: offer your "little willingness" to see beyond the apocalyptic fear of judging our thoughts. This makes us ready to take our place in God's Plan of Atonement. When we have completed separating our thoughts, retaining only extensions of God's Love, there is no reason for fear to remain. Our sense of Self, our Christ Mindedness and love of others will change. Our belief in mankind and our relationship with God will be transfigured.

As our awareness of Heaven descends into consciousness, Christ will have returned. Jesus of Nazareth brought this idea of Christ into our Western conscious awareness 2,000 years ago. His presence is still in our mind. As the Elder Brother and Teacher, he extends his hand to show the pathway. The Second Coming will be Christ awareness in our own mind. Separated by a tiny gap, it will begin as each of us chooses with the Spiritual Eye or the Voice for God.

We have the key to Heaven. Our Elder Brother will show us how to bridge the tiny gap of separation. He only asks for our "little willingness" to complete this task. This is our part in The Plan of Atonement. This is God's Plan of Salvation. It is we who make The Last Judgment.

Chapter 5

The Anti-Christ,

The Second Coming and

The Great Crusade

The antichrist is the substance of nightmares, the evidence of fears unknown. Its manifestations are enemies unseen. Rooms grow silent at the mention of its name. Goose bumps rise on our necks. Images of a seven-headed monster emerging from the sea slither into our minds. This is the beast that will lead the battle against God's chosen people as he champions evil forces against good. Satan and the antichrist will unite in a last desperate assault on Christ and His church. These horrible thoughts are signs of "end times." They occupy our conscious minds, engendering fear which erupts uninvited.

Studied scholar, Robert Fuller, gives specificity to modern beliefs in the Apocalypse in his book, *"Naming the Antichrist."* His research identifies three central themes generally assigned to the antichrist:

- *Promising peace to those who follow, he will rise to a position of great power.*
- *With the help of his own false prophet, the antichrist will gain control of the world economy.*
- *Each person will be forced "to be marked on the right hand or the forehead, so that no one can buy or sell unless he has the mark, that is, the name of the beast or the number of its name ...666."*
- *One of the heads of the beast also "seemed to have a mortal wound, but its mortal wound was healed, and the whole earth followed the beast with wonder."*

These beliefs are in my unconscious mind. Those prescribing to a literal understanding of the Book of Revelation become targets of my sarcasm. Having dissociated my fear, I now blame them for consequential terror engulfing my world. This is an attack against my brothers; I have made someone else the cause of my own fear. I have judged him. He is found unworthy, and now I condemn him to eternal damnation. Fear is my protection. I now refuse to look at my alliance with this ego's thought system. As a built-in defense against the love of God, it ensures I will not recognize the Christ in myself via reflection in my brother. The mirror of salvation becomes dimly lit, blotted and now oblique. This is my dissociation, keeping me in everlasting damnation. This is the how our process of denial keeps us locked in fear.

Before dealing with the antichrist, we must expand on the concept of Christ. The term in Greek is "Christos," or anointed one. Jesus assumed the title of the "Anointed One." Charles Fillmore, founder of the Unity School of Christianity, suggested Christ is the mind of God, now individualized. I have found the Unity School's definition of the "Individualized Christ" a most reassuring concept. He and his wife, Myrtle, explained Christ is the life principle within each of us. We are the thought of God that has never left Heaven. Those who have individuated the ego have subjugated the ego-self to the higher Self. We will experience this individualized mind of God in conscious thought. My experience began with a different perspective.

Mary, Joseph and Jesus Christ

When I attended our local church as a child, I was taught Jesus Christ was the son of Joseph and Mary. Having not been told otherwise, I assumed his parents had the same last name as well. As their only begotten son, Jesus had no brothers or sisters, as far as we knew. We never saw pictures of his playmates or siblings. In our rural community, intellectual discussions on religion and philosophy were more apt to be found at the local tavern (we only had one). We had six churches, but Jesus Christ's name was proclaimed frequently at both – in different contexts, of course. Sometimes an "H" was added as a middle initial at the tavern. The Bible was to be read and accepted, not discussed or questioned. If it was good enough for King James, it was good enough for us.

Biblical discourse wasn't discouraged, but it wasn't a common practice. Reading it was even less frequent, and for good reason: missionary Baptists were more concerned with supporting missionaries in Indonesia than getting a last name correct. If you were told the Bible was inerrant, why waste time reading it? Actions were more important than words.

There were exceptions. For example, Macy was a revered member of our congregation. A retired school teacher, she had read the Bible cover to cover four times. She was an oracle. In the late 1950s, Macy was still driving a Model A Ford. Wearing a black hat and long dark dresses, her lace-up block-heel shoes showcased a broken ankle that had healed crooked, turning at a right angle. With age, her nose had turned slightly upward (viewed by a child looking upward) and developed the appearance of a split at the end.

When Macy rolled into church driving the Model A, cradled her Bible and began that splayed walk into the sanctuary, kids took notice. She was not an unpleasant person, but the aura of her appearance and this unmatched Biblical knowledge were captivating. Having read the Bible more times than most of our preachers, she sat with authority on her side of the aisle. If it was good enough for Macy, it was good enough for us. But from a kid's perspective, look what happened to someone who spent all their time reading the Bible: split noses, crooked ankles and Model A's!

Years later I enrolled in "History of the Old Testament" while attending our state college. My professor, a rabbi from Israel, had studied in London and was fluent in several languages. Not only could he read the King's English, he could read Hebrew as well. He clarified meanings in Hebrew from our text, The Jerusalem Bible, as we read in English. Three-fourths of the 30 students were also ministerial students at the three local fundamentalist Bible colleges across town. They had enrolled for an easy credit from the state college, their knowledge of the Bible being already inerrant. When the rabbi said we would start our study with Old Testament myths, we lost about half the class. By the time he defined myth as a literary term defining any story involving God or gods, another third had left the classroom. The six of us who finished the class found it to be a wonderful experience. Whereas before I had thought Pentateuch a chemical treatment for wooden fence posts, I now knew it as the Old Testament's first five books.

Unfortunately, I broke an ankle at a party and could not make the final exam (visions of Macy). I went to the rabbi's temporary house to present my class paper. We sat in folding lawn chairs in his relatively empty living room and discussed the Book of Ruth. It became clear to me scholarship and the search for meaning were the rabbi's foremost objectives, wherever they led him. As rabbi at the local temple and married to a college professor, he could separate his personal beliefs from studying history, theology and religion. His inquisitive approach to complex issues was a breath of fresh air to a mind stifled by blind acceptance of literal translations. It was comforting that a man of the cloth could hold an open mind while having intellectual discussions about matters of religion and theology. There was one issue; when I asked his thoughts about Joseph, Mary and Jesus Christ, the rabbi rolled his eyes and left the room.

Finding the Christ

One day, each of us will have to answer this question: "Who is the Christ?" The definition of the Christ can only be personal. If it is a reflection of the love of God in man, then could it be any other but our higher Self? Paul tells of two selves in Romans. His innermost Self is, in his mind, a source of Divinity he reveres. Paul then speaks of the slave self, which drives him to insanity. Yet a frequently quoted statement is attributed to Paul: "Christ in you, the hope of glory." He was indeed a mystery himself.

Augustine's studies of St. Paul combined with Plato's concept of "self or Self" influenced the Reformation movements in Europe. They also were instrumental to Freud and Jung in their research of the unconscious. From the latter two came such terms as "ego-self" contrasted with "Self," or, in this context, the Christ-Self. The latter applications are more in line with concepts presented by the author of "ACIM."

A would-be Saint, Origen of Alexandria – considered by some to be the intellectual father of Christianity – expanded on Paul's dilemma of dueling selves. Unlike Paul, he was more at peace as an outer image who saw things in a corporeal way, as well as the inner man who saw them from a spiritual perspective. Perhaps Origen's lack of conflict stems from a slight alteration. He had made himself a eunuch, as he felt instructed by the Book of Matthew. Later, he was declared an anathema and his writings were set aside by the Second Council of Constantinople in 553 AD. One can only imagine the state of Western Christianity had it followed Origen's writings, rather than those of St. Paul.

From an *"ACIM"* perspective, Christ is the enlightened or anointed Son. He is the presence of God in man, which is perfect and complete. This Christ-Self has never left our memory, our awareness of God, or His awareness of us. The author or Voice of the Course speaks frequently of the Christ. This begins in Miracle Principle No. 32, as follows: *"Christ inspires all miracles, which are really intercessions. They intercede for man's holiness, and make his perceptions holy. By placing him beyond the physical laws, they raise him into the Sphere of Celestial Order. In THIS order, man IS perfect."*

When Christ intercedes, we move beyond physical laws. We are raised into a higher sphere of Celestial Order, or that thought of Heaven already in our minds. This is the out-of-pattern sequence which moves us beyond time and space. When time collapses, givers and receivers of miracles emerge further along "in time." In this way, Christ functions in our lives. Like Heaven, Christ's perfection is a real thought in our minds.

Christ as Jesus of Nazareth

Traditionalists and fundamentalists contend Christ took form as Jesus of Nazareth. *"ACIM"* does not disagree. It suggests Christ is universal. It is not exclusive to any person or timeframe. Being collective in nature, it is both singular and plural. *"ACIM"* suggests Christ as Teacher and Savior will take many forms with different names. It will continue to appear until we can recognize those many names as only the One. This is an obstacle we must explore. The exclusivity of Christ to a single body, in a specific timeframe, is a point of contention. If Christ was limited to appearing in the Holy Lands 2000 years ago, can He be within each of us now?

I have used the terms "Christ-Self" in contrast to ego-self. These terms are more widely used in a psychological context than a Biblical application. I have assumed that self, when capitalized (e.g. Self) is synonymous with the Christ, as recognized by an individuated ego. This is the Son of God, no longer separated in our conscious mind. *"ACIM"* uses these terms interchangeably. They are synonyms for the perfect Divinity within every living thing. You may understand this as a thought or as our knowledge of Heaven in our mind.

Edward Edinger, MD (1946-1998), as noted earlier, was considered the dean of Jungian Psychology here in the United States and has written extensively on religious symbolism and the unconscious. He believed that many neuroses were associated with the decline of religion and the dominance of science. He thought it was important for the afflicted to grasp elements of religion, philosophy, literature and even alchemy to heal and thrive. In his work, "*Ego and Archetype.*" He defines Self as that archetype which orders and structures our conscious and unconscious mind. Self, when capitalized, should be distinguished from "self," which is a reference to the ego-self. His terms correlate closely with "*ACIM.*" Archetypes, in theory, are primordial patterns of living energy in our collective mind. They are universal and timeless. Dynamic and alive, Jung and Freud introduced these concepts as naturally reoccurring forms of living energy in our mind. Popular psychology gives archetypes names we can identify such as king, warrior, mother, scapegoat, hero, etc. They are the subjects of mythology, art and music, and include both Biblical and religious figures of all persuasions. We rediscover them and use new names in each generation.

Christ or Christ-Self is that part of our mind which has never left God. This is the Memory of God within, the central focus of our conscious and unconscious minds. This energy orders and structures our inner universe. It is the perfection in every living being. I may see the Christ through reflection in my brother. Behold, this is the Christ or Divine Self within you. The author of "*ACIM*" would suggest "within" is not necessary, the Christ is you. Christ is not a part of us hidden inside, but our true being. Everything else is of our own making, and not real in the eyes of God. As noted earlier, it is the whole being and its circumference.

Edinger suggests Jesus of Nazareth is one who came into full awareness of his Christ-Self. In so doing, he awakened the entire Western World. Just as miracles benefit sender and receiver, so did this awakening affect us collectively. It raised all of us to a higher level of conscious awareness, moving closer to understanding our true identity. Jesus' awakening to his Christ-Self was among the first "Speed-Ups" in the Western mind. This was the power of only one, acknowledging his reality, as the Son of God.

The Text's reference to Self can mean Christ in you, the reader. It may also mean our fellow students, individually and collectively. It is the inspiration and ultimate voice of the Course. This source of knowledge can also be understood as the author of the Course, or sometimes referred to as the "voice for God". As you read and study, a correct definition will be revealed. Seek your own. As understanding approaches truth, peace will harmonize like a perfect symphony. This is knowledge of the Christ. Peace is your validation.

Just as I project unconscious fear onto others, I can also project my Christhood outward. This is dissociation as well. By assigning Christ exclusively to an historical figure, such as Jesus of Nazareth, I successfully reject what God has created. Seeing Christ with the "Spiritual Eye" is different than projecting my divinity onto another. Sin, by definition in *"ACIM"*, disowns our spirituality. This is our belief in separation from our Christ-Self. Belief in separation is our only sin.

Religions based on morality are preoccupied with sinfulness. Sin is allegorical in the Old Testament, first appearing in Genesis as a serpent, and then as a vicious animal to Cain. Named sins are legion, such as the Seven Deadly Sins and the Ten Commandments; both define our sins of commission and omission. Sin fits the mindset of legalism struggling for power and domination, not forgiveness and salvation. Two thousand years of defining sin has not satisfied our craving for spiritual renewal, nor has it produced peace as a byproduct. We need a different perspective. According to *"ACIM,"* there is only one sin!

Sin as a Belief in Separation from our Christ-Self

Sin becomes a family lineage descending from the patriarch. Like a pedigree, we are focused more on its origin and application than its unreality. Sins of parents are visited upon the children, naming offspring to protect their heritage. *"ACIM"* will name only one sin – failure to acknowledge Christ within my brothers. As a reaction of our egos, it keeps us from comprehending our own divinity. Committed in the past, we revisit this decision every time we see someone as a body separate and apart from their Christ-Self.

"ACIM" tells us the face of Christ shines in each of us now. When we recognize this Christ awareness in our brothers, we see the reflection of our own Christhood incarnate. The Christ is directly in front of us. He is the one we see as a thorn in our side or our resentment de jour. Christ Vision is an awareness of the innocence in everyone we meet and in each person that comes into our mind.

Vision does not mean to see with physical eyes. It is an understanding communicated from our higher Self. Individualized for maximal teaching purposes, it may be visual, audible or intuitive. We will know this presence by the experience of peace in our mind. "*ACIM*" uses the metaphor of frame and picture to promote the inner imagery. We place a picture frame, in our mind, around the one we hate. The frame is a symbol of the ego and body we have made in our minds. The picture is the true Christ-Self. We confuse the two, seeing only the frame and not the picture. When we ask to see with the "Spiritual Eye," the picture is revealed in a veil of light. We see beyond the frame of a body which we created in our mind. If this happens in my mind, it can become external.

Lesson 121 (Forgiveness is the Key to Happiness) in the "*Workbook for Students, ACIM*" has a similar mental exercise. It suggests we make a mental image of someone whom we dislike, and then find a little spark of light in this perceived enemy. Expand this spark of light into a beam, and then include someone we love. That person now stands next to the hated one in the mind's image. As both stand completely surrounded within this beam of love and forgiveness, they extend their hands to us, offering this spiritual light in return. Seeing them both in a light of love and forgiveness, and not just as physical bodies, all happens in our minds. Our co-creations are extending the Love of God to us, in our own mind. These mental images become our Savior. When we are ready to forgive our protagonist, this exercise really works. We have made and named the images of bodies and extended the Love of God to each. Our creations have extended spiritual Love to ourselves. This is the process of forgiveness. It is complete when we experience a release of anxiety and receive peace of mind. This change in perception is the miracle and meaning of forgiveness. We need do nothing more. Forgiveness seeks us as well.

Learning to choose with the right mind takes practice. Outer forms offer deceptions. Repeatedly we choose with the wrong mind. We have hidden the Face of Christ in generations of resentment, fear and condemnation. We are unconscious of this presence. Our shroud of separation is given many names; some carry transpersonal energies of terror, disease, war and pestilence. They are veils appearing as shields.

What on earth could hide the Face of Christ? What dark sin or pagan idol could obscure such shining Light? How could Heaven be in our midst and not be seen? We have created a horrific archetype to keep us in everlasting damnation, but can it separate us from our own perfection? This many headed monster with beastly marks leads us into mortal despair. Like Cain, we are banished to Nod, east of Eden. There we wander in desolation, trying to cast out what we have made to perpetuate our seeming endless separation. Heaven's release waits behind a false god we have forged into tiny molds of fear. What ingenious name could we give this idol? It now appears in the form of bodies or images of bodies our ego has made. It does not belong to one body but to all, for we gave it the perfect name – the antichrist.

The Anti-Christ is not external

"*ACIM*" tells of the true antichrist. It is an idol, nothing more. Idols are not recognized for what they are, because the powers we give to idols hide their true meaning. The purpose of an idol is to obscure. That is why we fear and worship them. We do not know what they are for or why we have made them. Idols may be a body, a thing, a place, a situation or a circumstance. They may be an object owned or wanted or even a right, demanded or achieved. It is all the same. An idol is the image of our fellow man that our mind has made.

Idols take deceptive forms. They are substitutes for reality. In some strange way, idols seem to offer safety in a world of danger. They supply our needs by adding value to the uncompleted. Idols have the power to enslave. They fix our vision on the external. If we only look outside, we never look within.

Enslaving ourselves to an idol is the penalty we impose for refusing to look upon our Divinity, the Christ-Self. These idols are more than just golden calves; they adorn a gap. False beliefs fog the space between our true reality and the fiction we have made about each other. The tiny gap is a void, awaiting our recognition and bridge. If Christ is our true identity, then any idol is an image or belief that opposes this truth. Its purpose is to obscure. The image I have made, in my mind, of my fellow man is the false idol. This must be our antichrist. Just as a cloud does not remove the sun, idols are only a temporary obstruction of light.

Likewise, an actor on stage is not his character. He is the person behind the makeup and costume for the one he portrays. Such are idols. Their sole purpose is to drape a veil across the Face of Christ. The Voice of the Course tells us the antichrist is a strange idea of a power that could surpass the omnipotence and omnipresence of God.

This insanity is a belief we could be separate and apart from our own Creator. It is a thought system that purports we created a world beyond the infinite. This is our concept of time that transcends Eternity. Here the world of idols has been placed. Here we have reinforced these ideas. Our thoughts of power and place are given form. Here we define and measure time to fit our needs. We have made and shaped a world where the impossible has happened.

Armageddon: Battle with the Self

The Battle of Armageddon will be fought in our own minds; it is the struggle for our Soul within. We are caught in tugging wars: the voice for the ego and the "Voice for God." Choosing to worship idols will join forces with the antichrist. This is battle against my true Self, the chosen One of God. But now I have another choice.

Today, I can choose to stand with Christ in Heaven where my true Self resides. No longer will I worship idols I have made. This is the decision against everlasting torment and terror to which I am so accustomed. I may recall my memory of an ancient melody, The Song of Songs, with a rhythm that reflects the Peace of God. This is the love I seek within. It is not that we are unaware of this memory, but we have chosen not to remember. This is an important distinction. All knowledge is in my mind; I am just denying my recall. So pervasive is my choice to not remember, I need help of a spiritual Teacher to make the decision.

We have drawn a veil across these memories of our Christ awareness. Our vision is dimmed, our hearing grown dull. As the ego shouts in our ear, "This beast from the sea has come to wage war in your mind,"... remain silent. Ask for vision from the "Spiritual Eye," ask to see beyond false prophecies. Do not be tempted by the devil in your mind; it is he who is the false prophet. These ego thoughts have turned our thinking "upside down." What is true appears false, the false appears true. I cannot tell Christ from its antithesis. This is work of the antichrist.

"Then I saw a beast coming from the sea, having ten horns and seven heads, and on his heads were blasphemous names."

--Book of Revelation

The emergence of the antichrist as "a beast from the sea" is our resistance to awareness of the Self. This is the Christ who has promised he will come again physically in a body, but also as conscious awareness in every mind. We experience this as light and living energy.

In the Apocalyptic Myth, the antichrist emerges to begin the last great crusade. In mythology and dream interpretation, the presence of water symbolizes our unconscious mind. Something emerging from the sea would imply an image or symbol from our unconscious, of which we are not aware. Before we can experience the coming of Christ to our conscious awareness, we must allow the blocks to be removed. These unconscious idols are the beasts which must come into our understanding. Once they come to our conscious awareness, we can give them to our spiritual Teacher for removal.

Many believe Jesus of Nazareth was the Course's author. The author describes himself as a disembodied spirit whom we can rely upon as if he were our Elder Brother. This teacher has overcome these false idols, the many beasts from the sea. Walking on water is symbolic of functioning at that level of higher learning referred to by Dr. Jung. Jesus lived out from the Christ-Self. One who can walk on water symbolizes one who rises above untrue thoughts in our unconscious mind. Jesus was identifying fully with the Christ-Self. When he was tempted, he could say, "Get thee behind me Satan" (the ego-self).

Buddha rode backwards on a water buffalo to symbolize overcoming the ego thought system. Jesus and Buddha are both symbols of enlightenment. They are great teachers moved beyond any hold of false idols. These teachers are also thoughts in our mind. We have access to their knowledge when we choose to listen with the facility of the Spiritual Eye, the voice or intuition in our right mind. Only a thin veil shrouds the Love of God. This is not really separation. It is little more than distance "in time" which drapes the fear of awakening. Fear foretells of our coming awareness, a rebirth. Ask the Spiritual Eye to set your thinking right. The Face of Christ shines so brightly it cannot be cloaked. We are given true vision to see beyond obstacles we have made, the beasts from the sea.

What appears as a rough scaly beast at first blush is not really a monster from the sea. Its true mission is to save us from our fear. We must surrender what we have made. It is our Savior who slouches as it slithers its way toward Bethlehem, awaiting rebirth and resurrection in our minds. This reflection is so bright it illuminates our brother's face like a bright star in the night. At last, its hour has come around. This is the blessed event for which we have been waiting. The Christ has come again.

The Second Coming

The first coming of Christ is another name given to our Divine Creation that has always been with us, even before time began. The Course's voice repeatedly tells us we are the Christ, the Son of God. The Second Coming means permanent awareness of Christ, or the Divine Self entering our conscious mind. It is the end of the ego's rule over the minds of men. This is the mind's Final Healing. The Voice tells us that He was with us in the first coming and He now calls us to join with him in the second.

In retrospect, we can review our lives and see how we have been carefully prepared for this awakening. The Voice tells us He is in charge of the Second Coming. Any judgment on behalf of God is used only for our protection; it cannot be wrong and it never attacks. Our judgments upon everyone, including ourselves, are mistaken. All have been chosen. Any attempt to reject or deny this choice is not humility, but the arrogance of our egos. The decision has already been made.

The function of our egos is to convince us only a few have been chosen. The Voice for God brings us this message of Truth: Christ is our true being. This is Reality. The Book of Revelation tells of the complete knowledge of our true Self. The Second Coming means Christ is coming into our minds to heal wrong thinking. The voice, or Course author, is working with our Higher Minds whether we are awake or asleep. This is an assurance.

"*ACIM*" suggests it only feels like we are being attacked, but Christ works with us as the part of our mind which knows the Truth. Meanwhile, our ego is working with the lower minds, giving us a false message of siege. In the end, we will join with the truthful voice in his "Great Crusade." This decision was made before we chose separation. Holding the hand of this Voice, we see jointly with the Spiritual Eye. Standing in the presence of the Christ Mind, these decisions make us invincible and eternal. They are metaphors for how we interact with an awareness of Christ in our mind during and after the Second Coming.

As the Love of God and the Presence of Christ become our conscious awareness, we are restored to sanity. This restoration could also be called "raising the dead," because we will know eternal life is an attribute of every living thing God created. As we accept our mantle of Christ, we can perform the miracles as assigned. Miracles are the change in perception, or a reconsideration of the false judgments we made of our fellows. No one reassessment is greater than any other, even though we believe this is true (the Course's voice and Spiritual Eye do not). Miracles are the natural profession of the Children of God. Our acceptance of this vocation is inevitable. This is our part in the Plan of Atonement, and it begins today. Armed with our true identity, our journey starts anew. Our burdens are now easy. Remember, our message is now Light.

The Great Crusade

"*ACIM*" explains the Atonement means to restore everything we think we have lost or restore it to our conscious awareness, for we never lost anything. "Atoning" really means "undoing." The undoing of fear is an essential part of our Atonement, the greatest value of miracles. When we restore our awareness to its original state, we become a part of the Atonement. The purpose of the Atonement is to restore to us everything we think we have lost. but it is really restoring our awareness. We have only mistakenly perceived what we think we don't have, for we have lost is not real. The Voice tells us we were given everything when we were created. As we are restored to recognition of our original state, we naturally become a part of the Atonement ourselves.

The Voice insists we will share his inability to tolerate a lack of love in ourselves and others. Having made this decision, we will join the Great Crusade to correct our thinking. It takes place in our mind, not on a battlefield. He even gives us a slogan for the Crusade:

Listen, learn, and DO;

Listen to his voice,

Learn to undo error in our thinking, then

DO something to correct it.

But what should we do?

I Need Do Nothing ... The Paradox of Miracles

But I must do everything; I must perform miracles.

Herein lies the paradox which holds the Peace of God. The power to work miracles belongs to each of us. The Voice will provide opportunities to work miracles. All we need to do is be ready and willing, because we are already able. Performing miracles fortifies our conviction in these new-found abilities. It strengthens through accomplishment. Miracles are part of the Atonement in this wise:

The ability is the potential;

The achievement is its expression; and

The Atonement is the purpose.

I need do nothing, but I must do everything.

A paradox offers apparent mutually exclusive options. Its beauty is found in the tension it creates between opposite polarities in our ego's thought system. When we hold this tension of opposing forces, we all rise to higher levels in consciousness. This is the "higher place of learning," holding new levels of understanding Jung referred to in his letter to Bill Wilson. The Voice of the Course will continually present us with paradoxes. The challenge is to be still, listen and learn to rest in the silence of "not knowing" the answer. Wait for your higher Self to present an answer. Remember, the voice of the ego seemingly speaks first because it speaks loudest. However, the very best our ego has to offer is hatred. Wait quietly; the right answer will come. First, it thunders in the silence. Then it resonates with harmony in our ears.

The presence of peace will follow with a rested assurance, and happiness and joy will ensue.

What is a Miracle?

Let's revisit this concept of miracles, as defined in "*ACIM*." Miracles are a change in our mind. They occur when we choose to see a person or situation differently through the faculties of the Spiritual Eye. The miracle is a learning device that lessens the need for time. The miracle implements a shift from the longitudinal or horizontal plane of perception to the vertical plane of perception. The doer and the receiver both emerge further along in time than would otherwise have occurred. In a visual sense, The Spiritual Eye is the vertical communications link between our little minds (the ego) and that higher place of learning in our right mind. It is wrong-minded thinking to believe we are separated from God; our Christ-Self knows otherwise. It is in our right mind where the Spiritual Eye resides awaiting our conscious decision to join. We must access this right mind to perform miracles.

This sudden shift in perception will question our belief that time is endless, that we must live under the laws of time. Miracles have the unique property of shortening time by rendering unnecessary the space time occupies. There is no relationship between the time a miracle occurs and the time it covers. It is a substitute for learning that might otherwise have taken thousands of years. It does this by the underlying recognition of perfect equality and holiness between the doer and the receiver. On this, the miracle rests.

The Voice of the Course has said that miracles abolish time. It does this by a process of collapsing time, thus removing certain intervals within time. This occurs within the larger temporal sequence. It establishes an "out-of-pattern" time interval not under the usual laws of time. Only in this sense, is it timeless. By collapsing time it literally saves time, much as daylight savings time does. It rearranges the distribution of light. The miracle is the only device which man has at his immediate disposal for shortening time.

Revelation transcends time. Our part in this Great Crusade is offering the "little willingness" it takes to ask the Spiritual Eye for a change in our perception. As noted in the beginning, the Voice will provide the opportunities to perform miracles. We need only ask: What miracles should I perform today? I need do nothing more!

I Must Do Everything, I Must Perform Miracles

"ACIM" is a correction device for our Western ego mind. We as a society are preoccupied with discovery of scientific knowledge. It strongly reinforces our ego thought system, keeping us believing that we are separate minds as individuals. We must protect ourselves from all attackers. As this belief becomes more invincible, we refuse to look or even reconsider our precious scientific knowledge that is the cornerstone of the entire ego thought system. The great awakening of the Middle Ages, brought about by rational thinking, improved our living condition. It also inflated our ego minds to the state of extending beyond knowledge of our Christ-Self. Instead of returning to the Garden of Eden, we travel further away from awareness of our Divinity, in time.

We are plagued with our mastery of the scientific process: propose a hypothesis, conduct research, verify data and reach conclusions before making decisions. Abraham Maslow once said the scientific process takes people of no value and gives them worth. He was referring to the lack of original, intuitive or creative thinking the scientific process supplants. Cultures not accustomed to this process use a more primitive means of thinking that carries the same name. This primitive method does not follow this logical format. The primitive reasoning is much closer to that "higher place" of learning in our right mind. With fewer cultural blocks, their decisions tend to flow with intuition. Jung observed this process while visiting Native American tribes here in the United States and also on his travel to Africa. He details these findings in his autobiography, *"Memories, Dreams and Reflections."*

Jung called this primitive reasoning accessing the "primitive mind." His comment was tongue in cheek, as it is not primitive at all. The primitive mind is in fact a thought system still aware of higher levels of consciousness that those with scientific persuasions have forgotten. Stated in *"ACIM"* terms, we have chosen not to remember. Unlearning an automatic response to our ego's logical thought system is essential in hearing the voice that will choose for God and for us. A little willingness to hear this voice is the "everything" I must do. This is accepting my place in The Plan of Atonement.

Projection is an unconscious choice for guilt, followed by choosing fear with our ego minds. We project this outward onto our brothers. Next, we look for messengers to confirm our decision. Rather than look at our decision to choose guilt and then fear, it is easier to assign cause to someone outside, someone other than ourselves. Once I choose fear, I send out messengers to find shame. "*ACIM*" teaches us this is an attack on ourselves we project onto our fellow man. We do this individually and collectively. It occurs culturally, politically, and in every other aspect of our lifestyle. This is an act of dissociation. This is the part of my ego thought system that maintains separation from the Christ-Self. This keeps me in an everlasting state of hell.

The Not-So-Great Crusade

Around 950 AD, the good monk Adso penned his epistle, "Letter on the Antichrist," which was widely disseminated throughout Europe. Adso's letter established today's widely held belief in apocalyptic thinking. He predicted the ultimate destruction of our modern world, and he is credited with formulating ideas of uniting Christianity in a holy war against the Muslims. At that time, Jerusalem and the Holy Lands were under Islamic control.

A few centuries later, Joachim of Fiore, a 12th Century monk from Italy, connected the Book of Revelation with the End of Times. He offered a view of history in three eras associated with Christianity's Holy Trinity. The Father, he said, is the time of Old Testament or Law. The Son is related to New Testament or Gospel. The Holy Spirit, or third era, will appear after the antichrist in a period of Enlightenment.

Joachim's prophetic vision of the Second Coming named Saladin, then the current Islamic leader, as antichrist. Saladin retook the City of Jerusalem from the Crusaders in the year 1187. Joachim's international reputation made him an apocalyptic advisor to popes. Perhaps more important was his advice to King Richard the Lion Hearted. On his way to the Great Crusade, King Richard spent the winter in Italy seeking council with Joachim.

This intermingling of fear, politics, religion and holy war over divine real estate has fermented for centuries in our conscious minds. It remains the center of world conflict today. Rest assured, if a sufficient number of Christians see the Islamic world as host to the antichrist, equal numbers hold opposing beliefs in the Islamic mind. Each of us now marshals forces of good to fight evil in the Battle at Armageddon. We are on a holy but perilous course, each believing God is on our side. It is like a duel to protect the honor of our individual beliefs.

A collective choice for fear evolves within each of our unconscious ego minds. It engenders tremendous transpersonal energies. We project attacks on each other. Both cultures wish to destroy the evil Satan. In reality, it exists in our individual minds. These are opposing "Calls for Love" on a collision course. The consequences are of apocalyptic proportions. This is a paradox of destruction. Fortunately, there is another way.

What follows are excerpts from a letter by Edward Edinger, written to his Los Angeles newspaper in response to the Oklahoma City bombing, the fiasco at Waco and accelerated acts of terror around the world. This letter was written on September 11, 2002, but never published:

The Psychology of Terrorism

Terrorism is a manifestation of the psyche. It is time we recognized the psyche as an autonomous factor in world affairs. The psychological root of terrorism is a fanatical resentment, a quasi-psychotic hatred originating in the depths of the archetypal psyche ... carried by religious (archetypal) energies. ... terrorists generally express themselves in religious (archetypal) terminology. The enemy is seen as ... the Principle of Evil (Devil) and the terrorist as "heroic" agent of divine or Objective Justice (God) ... which temporarily grants the individual almost superhuman energy and effectiveness.

These individuals are not (necessarily motivated as) criminals and are not madmen although they have qualities of both. Let's call them zealots. Zealots are possessed by transpersonal, archetypal dynamisms deriving from the collective unconscious. Their goal is collective, not personal. The criminal seeks personal gain; not so the zealot ... In the name of religion or "patriotic" vision ... they sacrifice their life in service of their "god." Although idiosyncratic and perverse, this is fundamentally a religious phenomenon that derives from the archetypal, collective unconscious. Sadly, much needed knowledge of this level of psyche ... is not available. Edward M. Edinger, MD

This transpersonal or collective unconscious cannot be understood or properly corrected by our conscious ego minds. This constellation of fear and zealotry is manifested as the "Archetype of the Apocalypse." Dr. Edinger used this phrase to describe the transpersonal unconscious energy that enthralls groups and cultures. When fixated in its grip, it is almost impossible to escape the effects. We must have help from another source, another thought system. The other thought system is accessed by the internal Teacher "ACIM" calls our Elder Brother. This is the part of our mind that accesses the enlightened or Central Archetype that orders and structures our being. This Christ-Self or Christ Mind is the universal collective Divinity we each share. It is individualized in our own minds. By study and acceptance of "A Course in Miracles," the individuation process is initiated and this facility descends into our conscious awareness.

Is it possible to live out from perception of the Christ-Self? As the frequency of choosing with our right mind increases and as we learn to listen for the Spiritual Eye within, the resistance becomes lessened. As more come to see this as our only choice, we literally do awaken collectively; the Christ comes again into our consciousness. This is the message of the Book of Revelation.

Christ is Coming Again: The Rapture

"ACIM" is only one of many pathways to individuation. It uses terms and concepts familiar to Western Christianity. Reading "A Course in Miracles" will maximize the individual's learning experience. As more join to read and study, the process accelerates until a critical mass is attained. We need do little more than offer the "little willingness" to change our own mind. Our little willingness is offered by acknowledging our denial of the "unwillingness" to listen to the Spiritual Eye. This begins the process. Next, open the text and join with others. Read one paragraph at a time; your internal Teacher will take over the curriculum. This is your pathway to awakening the "unlearning" process. The rest will follow. As you read, ask the Spiritual Eye for corrected perception about the judgments you have made on your brothers, the one in front of you or the ones occupying your waking mind. Either one will do. These are the judgments we have made on ourselves and projected onto each other. This is Holy ground on which we stand. Now it is fertile soil, seeded with miracles.

When opportunities for forgiveness are presented and we respond with an "act of Love", time collapses by thousands of years. Both sender and receiver emerge further along "in time." As the number choosing to perform miracles increases, the reduction in time becomes exponential. Just as a tsunami collects force in moving, our belief in and fear of death from an apocalyptic hell zooms right by us. We will see the unreality of fear as we acknowledge the reality of the Face of Christ. It now shines in what we formerly called our enemy. You are both reborn. This is the Rapture.

What is Holy ground, *"where an ancient hatred meets a present forgiveness?"* *"ACIM"*

Dr. Edinger offers an answer to Carl Jung's question of our survival as a world. This is the dilemma posed in his letter on terrorism. Like Jung, he responds yes: "Mankind will survive, but only if enough of us do our inner work!" Forgiveness is our inner work. We accept self-forgiveness by forgiving our brothers in our own minds. We must forgive them for what they have not done. Simultaneously, forgiveness is given us as well. This is the Second Coming, not just a historical Jesus in a physical body, but our conscious awareness of the Christ-Self bringing love and forgiveness as permanent resident thoughts in our conscious minds. This is the everlasting Christ, the only Son of God.

Here is the quote from Dr. Edinger again as he speaks of the Apocalypse:

"The coming of the Self (Christ-Self) is imminent; and the process of collective 'individuation' is living itself out in human history. One way or another, the world is going to be made a single whole entity. But it will be unified either in mutual mass destruction or by means of mutual human consciousness. If a sufficient number of individuals can have the experience of the coming of the Self as an individual, inner experience, we may just possibly be spared the worst features of ... manifesting the Apocalypse collectively and concretely in its most extreme forms." Edward Edinger, MD, *Archetype of the Apocalypse*

What is a sufficient number to sustain the awakened Christ in collective consciousness? The Book of Revelation hints at the number 144,000, but are we to take this literal or symbolic as a number of completeness. Both Edinger and Jung suggest only one is enough to awaken. Jung suggests Jesus of Nazareth was the first manifesting complete understanding. Edinger suggests Jung was the second. That is sufficient, Christ has only one Self. Our key is the "little willingness." Our Elder Brother and the Spiritual Eye both stand with us and at the "time end" awaiting our arrival. When we appear at the "end of time," God takes the last step into Heaven. This is the Celestial Sphere where we find eternal peace of mind.

In reality, this awakening has already happened. We tarry "in time" awaiting a sufficient number to recall our memory of completeness until we can overcome our ego's thought system. As this knowledge moves from intellectual to experiential awareness, the Celestial Speed-Up will accelerate. Our understanding of what appears to have happened long ago, "in time," will become present and immediate. Christ will have come again.

Chapter 6

The Voice &

The Transfiguration

The Voice and the Celestial Speed-Up

Who is the voice of *"A Course in Miracles?"* Dr. Helen Schucman and Dr. William Thetford asked the same question. Divine mind, Christ-Self, Jesus, Holy Spirit, Spiritual Eye ... are all names given to what some call Emanuel or God with us. It presents itself to each in different forms and names. Helen was quite disturbed by the dreams and visions she was experiencing before agreeing to take notes. Fortunately, she was a teaching psychologist in a medical research setting. Rather than declare insanity, Bill encouraged Helen to engage the experience. Before receiving dictation, she asked, "Why am I being asked to takes these notes?" One answer, as noted earlier, has been recounted by Kenneth Wapnick, Ph.D., in his book, *"Absence from Felicity."* In answering Helen's question, the Source indicated people were losing more than they were gaining, which necessitated a "Speed-Up." Certain people were going to be called back into this stratum of existence to lend their talents to God's Plan for correction. Bill and Helen's part in the Plan was scribing *"A Course in Miracles."* They were referred to as "Special Agents" with a mission.

Helen indicated the term "Celestial Speed-Up" was given to her, but never explained from whom. As noted earlier, Hugh Lynn Cayce suggested more than one voice channeled *"ACIM"* to Helen. Since "Celestial Speed-Up" is used only in the first four chapters of the pre-edited text, we should assume this was the other voice never identified by Helen. Many are uncomfortable with the concept of channeling from a divine source. Most of our traditional Western religions believe truth was channeled only once: 2,000 years ago. This belief is more a recent phenomena, strongly influenced by literalists and fundamentalists. Any means of correcting a mistake in Biblical transcription or interpretation would shake the foundations of inerrancy, long used to support social and political agendas. This has not always been the case.

Spiritualism, or divine channeling, was quite popular at the turn of the 20th Century before falling out of favor with mainline religions. Speaking in tongues has always been an integral part of Pentecostal evangelism. Many believe this a legitimate means of God's communication with believers. Unfortunately, no one can understand these transmissions because of the unknown tongues. "*ACIM*" suggests God will speak through many teachers and in many tongues, until they all become one. Metaphorically, the concept of God speaking to believers in unknown tongues would imply that truth is being spoken; we just can't hear the message. We do not have ears to hear or language to speak the truth. "*ACIM*" would agree with this. We have made a decision to hear from another voice in our mind, and chosen not to remember our choice for the ego. We refuse to listen to the Voice for God.

Many are skeptical of "*ACIM's*" nature and source, as I was myself. However, even a cynical disbeliever surely would question this position after reading the entire 600-page plus text, 365 "*Daily Lessons*" and "*Manual for Teachers*" without believing it had some means of divine inspiration. After understanding Helen and Bill's backgrounds and their skepticism of religion, it becomes difficult for a rational mind to reason otherwise. One can conclude "*ACIM*" had a divine inspiration, whose source or sources gave Helen and Bill the content for refinement and publication. Fortunately, the Author– or Authors – give clear understanding about its purpose. It is a plan for correction.

The Plan is God's Plan of Salvation. In that Plan is a "Voice of Truth" that speaks to each of us, both individually and collectively. What to call the Voice and how to honor "It" has been the subject of religious wars for millennia. "*ACIM*" constantly reminds us that words are but symbols of symbols, twice removed from reality. This is the ultimate knowledge of God. Any name given to this internal voice is nothing more than a symbol of a symbol, serving its purpose to awaken our Christ-Self within. Debating the outer form is useless. Like the Christ, It will continue to have many names until we can see only one. You may call symbols images of images as well.

A Symbol

Carl Jung's definition of symbol fosters an understanding of this point. He purports a symbol to be:

"An outer appearance of an inner awareness

that cannot otherwise be understood."

Symbols are different than signs. A sign is like a red traffic light, a universal stop. This is objective knowledge, dead to any subjective meaning. Dr. Edinger suggests symbols, unlike signs, have subjective meanings that connect us to psychological states which can affirm life. Words are not traditionally thought of as symbols; however, words represent images and images do carry subjective meaning, such as an image of the Virgin Mary. It awakens a state of awareness in our minds that we would otherwise not experience. It connects us to meaning hidden deep within the unconscious.

What we see with our physical eyes or hear with our physical ears is this outer appearance of symbol. The image as observed by our conscious mind activates and releases archetypal energy from our unconscious mind. What comes forth is experiential. We experience a conscious understanding that would otherwise remain beyond our recall or awareness. A symbol is not a sign post pointing in a direction; rather, it activates a numinous experience that transcends time and space. It moves us beyond our point of encounter. Symbols have the power to enthrall, but signs do not.

Some find symbolic figures or experiences in art, music or religious icons. Many find it in the rituals of Mass or the Eucharist. Others find it in nature, in tranquil settings or awe-inspiring landscapes. Those who experience this presence find that it is not easily forgotten. The Text will remind us that once such awareness is in our conscious memory, the "experience" is always subject to recall. This is our introduction to the voice "for" God. This is the beginning of our individualized Second Coming.

Helen experienced great trepidation when scribing *"ACIM."* She was reluctant to take dictation from an inner voice. *"ACIM"* calls this link with Divine awareness the Spiritual Eye. This term is used throughout the Text's first four chapters; it was later changed to Holy Spirit as in the context of Christianity's Holy Trinity.

The Spiritual Eye is defined as a direct communication link between us and God. This is a vertical connection between our conscious awareness and Divine Presence. Communication always flows to us, not from us. We contrast this with the "physical eye" or, in psychological terms, the ego. This "wrong voice" brings only anger, anxiety, fear and depression; hatred is its peak. While they may appear as polar opposites, in reality, the right mind or Spiritual Eye is the only one that communicates with our higher or Christ-Self. Non-dualistic thinking would say only the right mind is real. Like a movie projected onto a screen, the images are not real; they are light cast through a film. So is the world we create with our wrong mind. Our mind is the projector, the world is our screen. When images are given to the Spiritual Eye, they are transformed and can be used as our maximal learning experiences.

The Spiritual Eyes of God

References to Eyes of God or the Spiritual Eye are older than written word. These terms appear throughout the Christian Bible's Book of Revelation. The use of eyes as a spiritual symbol is also in Egyptian mythology. As noted earlier, the eye above the pyramid has its modern origins in Masonry. In the context of the *"Course,"* this is a communication link with God which is vertical, not horizontal. According to *"ACIM,"* the Spiritual Eye is the only part of the Holy Trinity that is symbolic.

The physical eye or ego appears to always see or speak first, and is always the loudest. Consequently, to hear and see correctly with our spiritual facilities, we must choose again after each perception. Our default mechanism is with the ego, but this can be unlearned.

Bill Thetford was not only Helen's supervisor, but as head of the School of Psychology at Columbia Medical College of Physicians and Surgeons, he was responsible for research projects. Some of his projects dealt with parapsychology, which led him into contact with the activities and readings of 20th Century psychic and mystic Edgar Cayce. Bill understood Cayce and Helen each had special talents: clairvoyance and clairaudience forms of channeling. Both found their special gifts disturbing and were reluctant to engage them. They were unsuspecting beneficiaries of their talents, using them as their part in the Plan and this current "Speed Up." Cayce had access to a memory bank that spanned generations of knowledge on many topics, of which religion and metaphysics were only two. Helen's gift was much more focused on the teachings of Jesus of Nazareth and psychology.

It was at Bill's insistence that he and Helen visited Virginia Beach, home of the Association for Research and Enlightenment (A.R.E.), Edgar Cayce's library and foundation, to present a copy of the scribed Text to Hugh Lynn Cayce., his son and head of A.R.E. Bill felt it important to seek the younger Cayce's guidance and counseling on "*ACIM*'s" deeper meanings. Dr. Kenneth Wapnick, the Editor of the first published edition of "*ACIM,*" recounting conversations with Helen and Bill about their meeting with Cayce, indicated he suggested more than one source or Voice was involved in presenting the Course to Helen and Bill. Since Cayce found different styles in writing between the first four chapters and the remainder of the Text, he offered the explanation of two distinct Voices dictating the Text. In the original manuscript of "*ACIM*", called the Urtext, which preceded the Hugh Lynn Cayce Version left at the A.R.E. Library, there was a considerable amount of information about Edgar Cayce and the Celestial Speed-Up. The elder Cayce had a significant part in this Celestial Speed-Up according to the Urtext.

Dr. Wapnick became "*ACIM*'s" editor and his recollections are available in many publications; one, "*Absence from Felicity,*" recounts the process and history of scribing "*ACIM.*" He met Bill and then Helen, who presented him with a copy of the Text. His tireless efforts in scholarship and editing must be commended.

When Helen began scribing "*ACIM,*" apparently neither she nor Bill expressed comfort with the term Holy Spirit. Consequently, the author used metaphysical terms such as Spiritual Eye in dictating the Text. This is a classic example of how the Divine Presence within speaks to us in a voice and with terms we are willing to receive. A spiritual teacher meets their students where he finds them. He asks only for the "little willingness" to begin the unlearning. Some of us must commence at simpler levels. Accepting the Holy Trinity in one swallow can be difficult for the uninitiated, as it was for me. In fact, "*ACIM*'s" author indicates our understanding of the Holy Trinity is our way out of the thought system closely guarded by our ego in the wrong mind.

Wapnick, in his own recollection, tells half-jokingly he suggested to Helen that she ask Jesus to re-dictate the early chapters. Realizing this was not going to happen, he and Helen did the best they could by editing the first five chapters so they could be integrated in the remaining text with common terms and symbols. Apparently the second Voice, which dictated the largest portion of the Text, felt it best to standardize rather than integrate the terms.

My first reading of the Spiritual Eye text was a breath of fresh air. I was then a confirmed Episcopalian with an understanding of the Holy Trinity in a liturgical context, yet I could not reconcile this with my metaphysical studies. It took years of reading to rid myself of preconceived notions in my mind, which was filled with fundamentalist teachings about the Holy Spirit, Jesus Christ and Devil. I assigned meanings to these symbols of Christianity, but they were evoking the wrong experiences. I was choosing with the wrong mind.

"And in the streets: the children screamed,
The lovers cried, and the poets dreamed.
But not a word was spoken;
The church bells all were broken.
And the three men I admire most:
The father, son, and the holy ghost,
They caught the last train for the coast
The day the music died."

Don McLean, American Pie

The Father, Son and Holy Ghost

One of my significant experiences with the Holy Spirit came in conjunction with my studies for confirmation at the Church of The Transfiguration, an Episcopalian church in Dallas. Prior to joining a liturgical denomination, I intellectually understood *"ACIM's"* definition of the Holy Spirit as a communication link with God. Further, I could see the Jesus of the Course as a self-described Elder Brother. However, these were mental understandings from my *"ACIM"* studies, not experiential. I harbored a tremendous resistance to a personal spirit; I was much more comfortable with a broad, numinous spirituality that encompassed everyone. It was during the Eucharist, while receiving communion from a priest (and a friend) that the presence of the Holy Spirit (or Spiritual Eye) became a living reality. This awareness of the Spirit as a communication link became a real experience, not an intellectual concept. In retrospect, this experience had come into my consciousness awareness previously during other religious settings.

Prior to confirmation as an Episcopalian and while traveling to New Orleans, I visited the Basilica in Jackson Square to observe a twilight Catholic Mass. It was attended mostly by street people. I was there out of curiosity, but I wasn't sure about the rest of the congregation. They looked more like a menagerie than a flock, fresh as they were from the French Quarter. Equally distracting was a well-dressed lady who dropped an ear ring; she spent the entire service crawling on her hands and knees under the pews. I assumed she was trying to find her ear ring; I was not sure what I was trying to find. Her lack of interest irritated me to no end. My attention was divided between the lady on her hands and knees, the street people fussing with their bundled worldly belongings and the constant coming and going of the remaining confessants. This was God working in my life.

The service's crowning glory was the priest himself. This weathered soul had a beet-colored face set against shiny white hair. His voice was raspy, with a slight rattle. I suspect he had imbibed more than once on Bourbon Street, which backed up to the Basilica. Spiritual messengers will arrive in out-of-the-way places with strange faces. However, all my distractions became invisible when the priest said, "If you remember nothing else from this service, please remember these three words: Come, Holy Spirit."

I was dumbstruck. Suddenly, I understood what he had said. I had found this new understanding of which he was speaking. An intuitive awareness flooded into my awakened consciousness, replacing the intellectual concepts I had been studying in "A Course in Miracles." I realized the Holy Spirit was a living energy or spirit. This is what others were experiencing in the ritual of Communion. No longer was the Holy Spirit an image of Casper the Friendly Ghost or even the Ghost of Christmas Past. In my rural Missouri community, the Holy Ghost possessed people, causing them to roll on the floors or speak in tongues. They were commonly referred to as "holy rollers," but this was something different. Like the lady searching for her ear ring, I, too was searching for something of great value: ears to hear. Fortunately, I only had to become willing to stop. Stop resisting and accept the presence. This congregation became my most welcomed messengers and saviors.

Breakthroughs are an integral part of the continuing individuation process. Dr. Edinger gives an excellent explanation in his work "*Ego and Archetype*," graphically depicting how our egos become alienated from the Self and swing like a pendulum between inflation and deflation. At times, the Self will metaphorically drop down and shock us into awakening. The nature of these awakenings is unexpected and sudden. It is in the seeking that we find. Jung states it better in "Synchronicity:"

"New points of view are not as a rule discovered in territory that is already known, but in out-of-the-way places (or experiences) that may be avoided because of their bad name (or undesirability)."

Devonshire in the West of England

My other experience with the Holy Spirit was more gradual in nature. It started at a former Benedictine priory in Dunster, County of Devon, in the West of England. I was traveling on business to London in 1992, and took a diversionary trip to the counties of Devon and Somerset for fishing and exploring. Purely by accident, I found lodging in the ancient Benedictine Priory, which consisted of an abbey, walled garden and dovecot, all built in the 13th Century. Next door was St. George's Church, with its traditional sanctuary, cruciform, high ceiling and choir screen. It housed two caskets holding the final remains of local crusading knights. There was also a wooden partition in the church to separate the monks from parishioners, as they were "annoying" to each other. Sitting in the church in meditation, I began to experience an awareness akin to that which bolted into my consciousness in New Orleans. Similar yet different, this became a gentle understanding accompanied by a continuing curiosity that was not easily satisfied. It took me some time to understand what was happening.

Edgar Cayce, in his discussions on metaphysics, suggests the true message of Christianity has been lost through many centuries of socialization and political influence. His suggestion, as revealed in his readings, is that any remaining "truth" in modern Christianity must be discerned through the architecture of traditional church structures. In other words, the English and European traditional cathedrals' shapes and layouts are symbols. Like an icon, the church structure as symbol evokes spiritual archetypes associated with traditional Christian names. These awakened living meaning as content of the Self, Central Archetype of our being. If Cayce is correct, this is the source of the Truth or knowledge to be found in modern Christianity. If a structure is a symbol, then it brings forth the experience of truth from our unconscious that we could not otherwise experience. The outer symbol brings forth our inner new awareness. As archetypal images, these structures induced a spiritual awakening.

Many European cathedrals were constructed over several decades by skilled masons, initiates of the ancient orders who found their origins in Egyptian mythology. The Masonic mysteries descended from the wisdom of King Solomon and the priestly Jewish communes that spawned early Christianity. The masons' vocations were more than just a way to earn a living. These builders were on a mission to raise structures that would hold understandings of the ages. More than mere buildings, these structures are vessels for spiritual knowledge. Like modern-day Masons, they were also building internal structures as temples for the spirit.

How does a structure carry a message of Truth which otherwise has been lost? I later visited the ruins at Glastonbury, site of England's first Christian church, where I also drank from the Chalice Well. In London, I visited the Knights Templar Chapel, Westminster Abbey and the St. Paul's and Winchester cathedrals. I found all of these to be awe inspiring, leaving with that same abiding curiosity. I have come to understand these visual experiences were a type of activating image which brought forth, into my conscious understanding, an inner awareness of an unconscious Divine Presences that, heretofore, had not been experienced. This was my mystery, contained in the architecture of ancient cathedrals, which activates energy in my unconscious mind. The cathedrals and icons are powerful symbols. Fortunately, they do not need to be analyzed when experienced; they are individualized experiences for personal learning.

A few years later, while reading Hugh Lynn Cayce's version of *"ACIM,"* I began to understand my dilemma. I had heavily shrouded my awareness of the Christ-Self. I was not willing to have it called forth by any source in my own mind. My fundamentalist upbringing's past images and experiences of Jesus and the Holy Spirit were clustered with these names. I could not see beyond the obstacles of guilt and shame I created to suppress the awakening experience. Words are only symbols of symbols. Our Elder Brother is one name for an internal spiritual Teacher. This is more prevalent in our Western mindset. The *"ACIM's"* Spiritual Eye or Holy Spirit is a vertical communication link with our universal Divinity. What we name them is only important to initiate our awakening to their presence. This is the purpose and process of reading *"A Course in Miracles;"* it will awaken the Divinity within, bringing it forth into conscious awareness. I had to "unlearn" my shame and guilt before I could realize that I was choosing "not to remember" the presence already in my mind.

Holy Spirit meets Holy Ghost

If the Holy Ghost is so significant in the Christian Myth, why do only Liturgical and Pentecostal sects see this presence openly engaged? Rational mainline churches seem less interested in a ghost being part of the Holy Trinity. Moralistic religions seem more interested in rules and their political ramifications. One must ask, Is this absence of celebration a resistance to the supernatural that cannot be rationally explained? In this frame of mind, faith in the unseen borders on the superstitious.

The Holy Spirit appears three times in the life of Jesus. His first appearance was with the Angel Gabriel to impregnate Mary, mother of Jesus. Second, it is witnessed by Jesus with John the Baptist and reveals, during baptism, his future vocation. Finally, 40 days following Jesus' resurrection and days after his ascension, the Holy Ghost returns at Pentecost, here referred to as the Paraclete. Dr. Edinger suggests this process is an "Incarnation Cycle," appearing as the birth of Christ and coming into our conscious awareness. It comes again as the birth of the church in the second annunciation.

In summary, the Holy Spirit, the Holy Ghost and the Paraclete are symbols of transformation reappearing from our unconscious mind. This is the Comforter which has come to show our way home, now reappearing in another format: the Spiritual Eye. However, the ability to perform miracles is not limited to a solitary son; this holy communication link is available to all who come with ears to hear. Like Jesus, we are baptized by the Spirit and have received a new vocation: the ability to perform miracles. We can change our minds by offering forgiveness. Remember, this is the miracle.

The *"ACIM"* process has applications far beyond Christianity. It suggests the outer image of our fellow man, seen in our mind, can become the symbol of the Christ within each of us. As noted earlier, a symbol is an outer image of an inner awareness that we cannot otherwise understand. We have made bodies, and they became our antichrist to shroud their true purpose. When we become willing to see with the Spiritual Eye, the image of a body becomes a symbol of the Christ. Rather than see attack or desire, we see an opportunity for forgiveness. Forgiveness is not reprieve, but a means of acceptance (I have misunderstood the true nature of myself and my brothers). We behold a body when in reality, the Christ presents Itself for our recognition. By offering forgiveness or the miracle, we shorten time. When a sufficient number initiate the process, the current "Celestial Speed-Up" will begin.

 "Closer than breathing, nearer than hands or feet," our Divinity awaits recognition in each of our brothers now. Yes Him, the one who is standing in front of us now. Yes, that one. He will do.

Spiritual Eye Choose for God, for Me, Today.

At every moment in time, we are at a point of choice. We either choose with the ego in our "wrong mind" or the Spiritual Eye in our "right mind." The right mind is that place of "higher learning" of which Jung spoke, home to the Spiritual Eye and our Elder Brother, or Teacher, who will show us our way. It retains memory of our divinity and awareness of the Christ-Self, which has never left the presence of God in Heaven. Our ego mind works like a default mechanism; it always chooses with the wrong mind because it appears to speak loudest and first. We must learn to consciously choose again, to choose the other way. Reading *"ACIM"* and completing the lessons is a retraining exercise that will begin to accomplish this end. The words, as symbols, will initiate the process.

When we choose with the Spiritual Eye, He will send out messengers to return affirmations of our choice. Among these are peace of mind, happiness, joy and forgiveness. The latter is the miracle. When we chose correctly, these are what we will experience. This is a promise. Choosing with the wrong mind or our ego attracts guilt; it is the decision we have for fear. It also has messengers. Like hungry stray dogs, fear will drag home guilt, shame and self-loathing for a feast of despair. We know we have chosen with the wrong mind when we are not at peace. Unfortunately, this "wrong" choice is made in our unconscious mind, of which we are not consciously aware. We only know it is the wrong choice when we feel the effects of anger, depression and despair. This is always our first choice; we must stop and consciously choose again before experiencing the Holy Instant.

Our minds must be trained to make this conscious choice at every point in time. Eventually, it may become automatic, but it first requires conscious effort. Continually choosing with the ego brings only depression and despair. The very best of ego is hatred with its many other gifts, and until we hit a brick wall of depression, we most likely have no motivation to choose again with the right mind. Each of us will come to a summit of life where things of the world no longer satisfy our craving for spiritual renewal. More money, another car, vacations, another spouse ... these will not satiate the pangs of hungry in our soul. This is the point of greatest peril. This is our opportunity to choose again.

The "little willingness" is our acknowledgement we really don't want peace of mind. Learning to offer this – and only this – to the Spiritual Eye is critical. Offering anything more will only retard our awakening. The Rules for Decision at the Text's end outline an excellent means for retraining the mind. It will not happen overnight, nor does a sudden breakthrough sustain the effort required to retrain our mind to choose correctly. It will take some work in the trenches to effect change, moment-by-moment efforts to retrain our mind and not just daily choosing. Submitting ourselves to this process requires maturity and a few battle scars. Our Day of Judgment has come. We must judge the ego in our wrong minds, for when we choose to climb to that higher place of learning, our lives become transfigured. We are like new wine; we cannot be poured into old skins. We are no longer captive to the smallness of our egos. We have gained Vision of the

Spirit. These are the "peak" or "oceanic" experiences that transform lives.

Discerning the Transfiguration

In the sanctuary of Dallas' Church of the Transfiguration, a large tri-fold painting renders an image of the Transfiguration. It depicts Jesus with Peter, with Moses and Elijah on the side folds as detailed in the Biblical story. I have always been enthralled by the story and symbols of the Transfiguration, yet have not found a satisfactory explanation within the traditional context of Christianity. It has significant meaning for "*ACIM*'s" students; I find this among the Bible's most important stories, yet it is seldom discussed and its meaning is obscure.

It is appropriate to approach the Transfiguration in context of awakening the Christ-Self within. This ability to see the Face of Christ in our brothers is mentioned only twice in "*ACIM*" (Lessons No. 124 and 151). Those transfigured have seen beyond the dark veil we have made to protect our true Christ-Self from recognition. This is the Rapture, the end result of the Second Coming. Having this experience is an apocalyptic nightmare for our egos.

Individuation, in Jungian terms, is the maturation process each of us eventually completes, coming into full awareness of our potential as spiritual beings, not just human beings. Dr. Edinger's work, "*Ego and Archetype*," has an excellent account of this self-realization or individuation process. This is an innate urge of life to realize itself consciously. It is transpersonal energy unfolding in our conscious minds to be used as an instrument to fully realize ourselves as the greater Christ-Self. The Transfiguration is the process of the Second Coming in our mind; it activates the ability to see Light in our brothers. (An excellent work on Jung's teachings about individuation and awakening to the unconscious is "*Inner Work*," by Robert A. Johnson.)

The Transfiguration's story holds great value in understanding our need to access a higher place of learning in our minds. As the story's focal point, this is seldom considered or discussed from a metaphysical perspective. For instance, Jesus is literally the Elder Brother, as characterized throughout "*ACIM*." An elder brother is one who has gone before us, has valuable knowledge to share and warrants our respect because of his understanding and experience. In "*ACIM's*" first chapter, the Author, or Elder Brother, tells us the only difference between him and us: we still believe we are physical bodies, not spiritual beings. That change in our self identification is the Transfiguration's mystery.

James and John

The Biblical account (The Jerusalem Bible) begins as Jesus takes his disciples – Peter, James and John – to the mountain top so they can be alone. They go to a "high mountain apart," this is the higher place of learning in their minds that Jung discussed with Wilson. As Elder Brother and friend, Jesus shows the way. Once there, he is joined by the presence of Moses and Elijah. We may think of them as the Elder Brothers of Jesus, his teachers and guides as well. Both Moses and Elijah had similar "mountain-top" experiences before they were enlightened or awakened to the Divine Spirit within themselves.

Once on the mountain top, Jesus becomes transfigured before the three apostles. They see his face and garments or his true Christ-Self, shining as with the light of the Sun. They could see beyond the body or "rays of darkness" (rays of darkness are "*ACIM's*" symbol of the body). Now they could see the Great Rays, as does the Spiritual Eye and as it will show each of us. A consistent symbol of our brothers' Divine Innocence is the Face of Christ and the message of Light; both are presented here. The disciples see with corrected perception, or Vision of the Spiritual Eye in the right mind, and behold the true nature of the Christ-Self. These concepts are presented and explained by "*ACIM.*"

A Lifting of the Veil

The Transfiguration can be seen as a "Lifting of the Veil;" the disciples now see to the past, symbolized by Moses and Elijah. They have moved beyond time and space to the higher place of learning, seeing through a veil of Light. Next a "bright" cloud appears. In dreams, bright clouds always foretell good things to come. The Voice speaks to them from the cloud in a commanding tone:

"This is my Son in whom I am well pleased. Listen to Him."

Affirming each have ears to hear, the Voice expresses the pleasure which God has with them and their Elder Brother. Note that there are seven if you include the Voice which is the Spiritual Eye or Holy Spirit, speaking to them from the cloud. Seven comprises the archetypes of three next to four which represents a synthesis into Wholeness or Christ-Realization for lack of a better term. Three symbolizes our becoming or transformation, while four symbolizes wholeness or completeness. Seven is also a significant number in the myth of the Apocalypse, which we will discuss later. When the Voice appeared, the disciples had a breakthrough; they saw the Face of Christ.

Jesus' Transfiguration takes place simultaneously in Jesus' and the disciples' minds. Jesus already knows he is Light, but in this higher place of learning, the disciples experience corrected perception. They are able to see a reflection of the Higher Self or Christ-Self from within themselves. This is the Rapture, as foretold in Revelation.

Peter asks if he should build alters (or tents depending on translation) for Jesus, Moses and Elijah. Jesus declines, asking not to be worshiped, and then reaffirms instructions from *"ACIM"*: He asks to be treated as an Elder Brother – worthy of respect for his knowledge and experience – but not held in awe. This should be reserved for God and Revelation, for which awe is appropriate. The only difference between Jesus as the Awakened Christ and us is we still occupy a body and believe it is our true identity. According to *"ACIM,"* He stands between us and God in a higher to lower order. He has one hand in Heaven and one hand in our world of the ego-thought system. He can lift us up when we cannot choose for ourselves.

The "Sons of God" Have Come

Continuing with the story, Peter asks Jesus about Elijah and the return of the "Sons of man." Traditional readings of the Bible take this to mean Jesus as the exclusive "Son of Man." Karl Jung, in his *"Answer to Job,"* devotes significant space to the Book of Revelation and specifically speaks to this phrase, "Son of Man." This term is used from the very origins of the Bible in both the Old and New Testaments. In some translations, "man" is considered a proper noun. Jung's assessment of the "Son of man" reference would imply it is not exclusive to the Bible's Jesus. *"ACIM"* references the phrase in a different context: the "Sons of God had returned.'"

The Jerusalem Bible's translation reads as if Jesus were not speaking of himself, but more in line with the idea of Christ-Self, the Divine "Son of Man" in each and every individual. I would suggest when Jesus advises the "Son of Man" has already come, he was not speaking exclusively of himself, but of the collective Awakened Christ in each of us. This is the first coming, a significant "Speed-Up" in God's Plan of Salvation and our pathway home.

Visualize if you can vials containing ocean water. Although they contain the same substance as the sea, they are no longer a part of the main body. The only characteristic for identification is the containers in which they reside. If you return the water into the ocean, its unique properties go away and it is united again with the whole. Such is the Christ, only our bodies and minds are the containers, not the content. Individuation or awakening the Christ-Self within is the process of bringing this into our conscious memory. Dr. Edinger refers to this emergence of the Self-ego axis, the connecting link to our Divine or Christ-Self as the significant point in our individuation.

Another way to view this awareness is in terms of a communication link between our smaller or ego-self and the greater Christ-Self that emerges into conscious awareness. This could also be understood as the Spiritual Eye's communication link to God. Christ is the ordering and structuring archetype of our being which has never left the memory of God. The communication link brings an understanding of this true Self into awareness. Our Elder Brother is the teacher in the conscious and unconscious mind awaiting our request for help. He will save us from our own condemnation and subsequent entrapment in this ego-thought system.

At points in his Transfiguration, Jesus is fully awakened as the Christ-Mind and no longer needs a body to function on earth. He is ready to cast his container aside. The Voice of the Course explains in "ACIM's" first chapter the difference between Him and us. He no longer has a body. Jesus has been transfigured into the Christ and has become completely identified with his Divinity. Karl Jung indicates spiritual awakening can be our greatest triumph, yet it is also a time of great danger, for we walk along the edge. Jesus was in this world, but said he was not of this world.

Four, Archetype of Completeness

Jesus and the three disciples, now an awakened foursome, or symbol of completeness, descend from the mountain. Jesus heals an epileptic boy whom the disciples could not heal, using the mustard seed analogy to identify the faith needed to perform miracles. This would be the "little willingness" which we should give to the Spiritual Eye, who then joins it with his greater willingness to perform miracles.

Jesus now has "corrected perception" as shown by his ability to heal. The disciples are conscious of the concept, but still unable to correct the perceptions; they have identified as and with the body and cannot heal. They have not yet been transfigured beyond time and space. Healing is the relinquishment of the thought we are in competition with God, or have killed God and must be punished. Sickness is one of our punishments. As Jesus, when we consciously realize and understand each of us is the "Son of Man" or Christ-Self, we are healed mentally.

Following the epileptic boys healing, Jesus has an exchange with a tax collector. Whom should we serve, he is asked, others and the sons of man, or the risen Christ within? Jesus implies it is futile to serve the ego illusions, which we have created in our own mind. We either choose with our Elder Brother and the Spiritual Eye in the right mind, or against them. Unfortunately, this is a black and white issue from an *"ACIM"* perspective.

Jesus instructs Peter to go fishing (exploring) and to take the first fish to rise, in whose mouth he will find a shekel. Water again is a symbol of our unconscious mind. The fish represents thoughts or divine ideas from the unconscious mind. Accordingly, the shekel is to be given to the tax collector for payment, which is analogous of being in the world, but not of the world. Similarly, we give all our worldly perceptions to the Spiritual Eye; those with Vision of the Spirit will be transformed. Our needs are provided as we accept our function in God's Plan of Atonement. Our function is learning to choose with the right mind by offering forgiveness.

As we learn to serve the Christ-Self, It instructs us on how to perceive our ego world of illusions. Instructions are given in this context: we must first ask the Spiritual Eye for our experiences' purpose. "What is this for?" We then ask to see them differently, invoking the process. Experiencing peace of mind is our affirmation.

I have spoken much of our concept of time and time coming to an end. I believe the Transfiguration's message is a precursor to our new relationship with time. When Jesus was transfigured, he remained in this higher place of learning in his right mind. He was identified with the Christ-Self. He could see the past and foretell the future, as he was functioning beyond time and space. While he still occupied a physical body, those with eyes to see saw him as Light or saw his spiritual body. He was able to heal, as with the epileptic, and teach, as with Peter and the fish. His final demonstration was power over the body, rising above death when crucified.

Perhaps the Transfiguration's message is this: the Second Coming is our awareness that death is not real, that we can live above time and space with authority over the unconscious mind and the ego. If water is a symbol of our unconscious mind, this is how Jesus symbolized walking on water. He functioned above the insanity of our ego-thought system. Our sustenance will come from Spirit, not man, and our antiquated concept of time is coming to an end. Time and the ego-thought system is now our servant, not master. The ego has subjugated to the Self.

Origen, the intellectual father of Christianity, writes of those transfigured as being awakened to the Word. The Word has becomes flesh or visible in the world to those who have eyes to see. He suggested that when we are transfigured by Christianity's message, we can read this message in any Bible verse. Forgiveness' message is now conscious in our minds. Transubstantiation would mean we see Christ's projection in every living thing. We will see this message in all those we meet, for Christ has been Transfigured into our conscious awareness – coming to remain this second time.

The Inflated Ego

Coming into this awareness is fraught with disaster. Our egos cannot resist an opportunity to inflate and take credit for the new awareness.

They extend their assumed authority beyond any circumference of self-awareness until pricked by a pin of the ego's reality, collapsing into a heap of depression. Jung refers to this as a period of deadliest peril:

"When we reach such a summit in our life, the solitary identity long enjoyed will exist no more; the one now becomes two. The greater figure (Self) which always was, but remained unconscious, appears to the lesser figure (the ego) with the force of a revelation! The small person will always attempt to drag the greater down to his littleness, never understanding his day of judgment has come. Those who understand this greatness will realize the long expected friend of our soul has come. The immortal one has come "to lead captivity captive" (Ephesians 4:8). When the (Christ) Self seizes hold of the little self (ego) and our life begins a reverse flow into the greater life, we are at a moment of great risk and in perilous danger." – Carl Jung

(Reproduced from "*Ego and Archetype,*" Edward Edinger, MD)

Many indicate the wish to turn back is overwhelming and, like Lot's wife, we will turn into a pillar of salt. This is the attendant who looked upon the Ark of the Covenant and was burned beyond recognition. Our Christ-Self's pure power needs the moderation of a right sized ego and an internal teacher able to respond to the awareness. Paradoxically, it is life-giving and life-taking.

Finally again like Job, we are the righteous man now totally deflated. We return to our dung heap to scrape our boils with shards of glass, to curse God and die. Job eventually awakened to the Higher Self, but only after great travails. His fourth friend, Elihu, became the messenger of synthesis or completeness. Would you rather be right or be happy? This is the question posed by "*ACIM*" and by Elihu to Job. Can the lesser self (ego) subjugate itself to the greater Self (Christ-Self) and live in peace? Each of us is faced with this quest of our inner work.

Edinger likens this self-awareness as our coming to an understanding: someone else is living in our house and making the decisions. As a matter of fact, these decisions are so effective we cannot even understand the genius until events transpire. In the mean time, we exhaust ourselves resisting a corrected path and attitude. Developing the right relationship with this emerging Christ-

Self is a lesson we will practice for the rest of our lives. Fortunately, a discussion group and compatriots on the same path will offer us valued assistance to dampen the swings between inflation and deflation that accompany the awareness. This is the pathway to the individuated Self. We need the support of others, but, we need to have a heart-to-heart talk about the crucifixion before we go one step further.

The Crucifixion to Reincarnation

The crucifixion is the single most important event in Western Christianity, besides the virgin birth. The spelling in my copy of the *HLC* version of the Text was cruci-fiction. The *"ACIM's"* Scribe, Helen Schucman, used this characterization in some editions. We may never know whether it was Helen's sense of humor or the author's; while not characterized this way in all manuscripts, the spelling was changed in the Course's published editions of *"ACIM."* I find the term very interesting. The insertion of fiction implies this may not have been a real event in the life of Jesus of Nazareth (I have added the hyphenation for emphasis).

The crucifixion is covered extensively throughout the *"Text, Lessons* and *Manual for Teachers"* in all versions of *"ACIM."* This perspective of Jesus' death supports a philosophy of non-dualistic thinking. A non-dualistic theology purports there are not parallel universes of Heaven and Earth, but only Heaven with Earth as a mental unreality created by us. It is unreal in the eyes of a Supreme Being and therefore not a part of God's creation, even though it appears very real to us. In this context, *"ACIM's"* author suggests too much emphasis is placed on "death," and not enough on resurrection. The crucifixion story takes place in an unreal world in our minds. The Course would indicate that what matters is that Jesus, as the awakened Christ, lived beyond time and identification as a body.

The *"Manual for Teachers"* also includes a discussion on reincarnation, which some find very disturbing. *"ACIM's"* purpose is to awaken us to our Christ-Self with the understanding that all of what remains is not real, and will be used only for this purpose. Accordingly, if a belief in crucifixion or reincarnation is necessary to facilitate this unlearning, then it becomes a part of our maximal learning experience. Some will find it worthwhile, some will not. That is a study group's purpose, to read and discuss these very issues.

Each student will find an answer that is satisfactory for their point in unlearning. The unlearning point is moving as each of us awakens. Today's beliefs in the unreal may not be relevant tomorrow.

One *"ACIM"* axiom is that words are but symbols of symbols, twice removed from our mind's reality. We each have sets of filters based on individual and collective experiences. We judge the present through these filters. Spiritual or metaphorical discernment is the ability to allow these outer symbols to activate an inner awareness that gives living meaning to our lives. *"ACIM"* speaks often of these differences: content and form, the inner versus the outer, objective or subjective. Content is another name for our living energy. The Spiritual Eye is our built-in facility to do just this, to discern Truth from untruth.

The Text's purpose is to teach others how to activate this capability and – even more importantly – to listen. The Course's Voice, the Spiritual Eye, is individualized so that a message with meaning to me may not be significant to others. A life-long Catholic would have found my experience in New Orleans of little value, if not rude. Perhaps western religions' greatest failings are an insistence on finding a "one-size-fits-all" answer to situations that require individual responses. While such an approach may have worked centuries ago, we now seek an individual relationship with our Christ-Self within.

Earlier, I quoted from Carl Jung's letter to Bill Wilson referencing the need to correct our upside-down thinking. Jung advises Wilson we each must walk a path that leads to higher understanding. Jung suggested we may be led by grace through contact with friends or a higher education of the mind. The Course's Voice suggests we relate to Him as if he were our Elder Brother, one with more experience who has gone before us in his unlearning. This is the most direct path to our levels of higher understanding that Jung suggests transform our thinking.

The following appears in the first paragraph of *"ACIM's"* published version and in the HLC edition's Miracle 48. Imagine someone speaking to you with specific instruction on how you are to think and go about accessing the Spiritual Eye. Imagine you are Dr. Schucman with a steno pad and pen, taking dictation that is not only personal to you, but for everyone who will read it:

"This is the invitation to the Spiritual Eye. I told you that I could reach up and bring the Spiritual Eye down to you, but I can bring Him to you ONLY at your own invitation. The Spiritual Eye is nothing more than your own right mind. He was also mine. The Bible says, "May the mind be in you that was also in Christ Jesus," and uses this as a BLESSING. It is the blessing of miracle-mindedness. It asks that you may think as I thought, joining with me in Christ-thinking. The word "know" is proper in this context, because the Holy Inspiration is so close to knowledge that It calls it forth; or better, allows it to come. The Spiritual Eye is the Christ Mind which senses the knowledge that lies beyond perception."

Upside-Down Thinking, Sex and the Distortions of Miracle Impulses

We each receive impulses to perform miracles on a continuous basis. Unfortunately, our ego receives the impulses and immediately distorts them for its own purpose before we even know they have been presented. This impulse has taken on a special form for moralizing religion, ensuring everlasting distortion, shame and self hatred.

If you were the Devil and wanted to hide a miracle, where would you place it? Where could you put a miracle so any God-fearing Christian would never find it, let alone look for its presence? What act creates shame and guilt within the American religious community to the extent it cannot be discussed by adults in open company? This subject is so taboo for teenagers we banish it to back rooms, alleys and the back seats of our cars. Rather than openly discuss a very important act, we avoid it. Of course, we are talking about sex.

The editors of *"ACIM"* made changes to the Section on the distortion of miracle impulses. The *HLC* Edition entitled the Section, "Sex and Distortion of Miracle Impulses." The editors changed "sexual impulses" to "physical impulses" in the published Text. Perhaps physical is more inclusive of our compulsions, but the Voice must have been clear to Dr. Schucman because she dictated "sex" in her notes for Dr. Thetford. What follows is the section copied from the *Hugh Lynn Cayce* Edition of *"ACIM."*

Distortion of Miracles Impulses

"You are involved in unconscious distortions which produce a dense cover over miracle impulses, and which make it hard for them to reach

137

consciousness. Any interpersonal relationship is limited or defined by what you want the relationship to DO. Relating is a way of achieving an outcome. The danger of defenses lies in their propensity for holding misperceptions rigidly in place. All actions which stem from reverse thinking are literally the behavioral expressions of those who know not what they do. A rigid orientation can be extremely reliable, even if it is upside-down. In fact, the more consistently upside-down it is, the MORE reliable it is.

However, reliability can only serve validity as the ultimate goal. Hostility, triumph, vengeance, self-debasement and other expressions of lack of love are often very clearly seen in the fantasies which accompany them. But it is a PROFOUND error to imagine that because these fantasies are so frequent that this implies validity. Remember that while validity implies reliability, the relationship is NOT reversible. You can be wholly reliable and ENTIRELY wrong. While a reliable instrument DOES measure something, what USE is it unless you discover what the "something" is? This course, then, will concentrate on validity – and let reliability fall naturally into place.

Miracle impulses' confusion with sexual impulses is a major source of perceptual distortion because it INDUCES, rather than straightens out, the basic level confusion which underlies the perception of all those who seek happiness with this world's instruments. Inappropriate sexual impulses – or misdirected miracle impulses – result in conscious guilt if expressed and depression if denied. ALL real pleasure comes from doing God's Will. This is because NOT doing It is a denial of Self. DENIAL of error results in projection. CORRECTION of error brings release. "Lead us not into temptation" means "do not let us deceive ourselves into believing that we can relate in peace to God or to our brothers with ANYTHING external."

Child of God, you were created to create the good, the beautiful and the holy. Do not lose sight of this. The love of God must still be expressed through one body to another because the real vision is still so dim. Everyone can use his body best by enlarging man's perception so he can see the REAL vision. THIS vision is invisible to the physical eye. The body's ultimate purpose is to render itself unnecessary. Learning to do this is the only real reason for its creation.

Fantasies of any kind are distorted forms of thinking because they ALWAYS involve twisting perception into unreality. Fantasy is a *debased form of vision. Vision and revelation are closely related, but fantasy and projection are more closely associated because both attempt to control external reality according to false internal needs. Twist reality in any way, and you perceive in a destructive fashion. . Reality was lost through usurpation, which in turn produced tyranny. I told you that you are now restored to your former role in the plan of Atonement, but you must still choose freely to devote yourselves to the greater restoration. As long as a single slave remains to walk the earth, your release is not complete. COMPLETE restoration of the Sonship is the only true goal of the miracle-minded.*

NO fantasies are true. By definition, they are distortions of perception. They are a means of making false associations, and obtaining pleasure from them. Man can do this only because he IS creative. But though he can perceive false associations, he can never make them real EXCEPT TO HIMSELF. Man believes in what he creates. If he creates miracles, he will be equally strong in his belief in THEM. The strength of HIS conviction will then sustain the belief of the miracle receiver. Fantasies become totally unnecessary as the wholly satisfying nature of reality becomes apparent to both."

I have reproduced this section on "Distortions of Miracles Principles" verbatim because it is easy to misunderstand or misrepresent the message. The "*ACIM*" published versions saw fit to change "sex" to physical. I can find no explanation for this other than the material's nature would have been far too controversial for1972, when some "*ACIM*" copies were first released.

The term "sex," like "Holy Spirit," brings a wealth of history which must be resolved for the Christ-Self to awaken in our conscious minds. While shame and guilt are universal, their effects are the same in a vacuum. My religious upbringing holds a special place for the wages of sex that promises a punishment greater than death: everlasting damnation. Until shame can be separated from sex and we see shame as a choice we make to keep us imprisoned in the ego thought system, we weaken our hope to awaken.

I included this excerpt from "*ACIM*" in total so you can see the Author's suggestions. Using our physical bodies as an instrument to express God's love is the best we can expect. Let me repeat it in case you missed the specific:

"Child of God, you were created to create the good, the beautiful and the holy. Do not lose sight of this. The love of God, for a little while, must still be expressed through one body to another because the real vision is still so dim."

The correct attitude would be to ask the Spiritual Eye for an impulse's purpose. This should be even more so if it causes us to feel uncomfortable. Our bodies have the purpose of making themselves no longer useful. When used for the ego's purposes, the body becomes a source of pain and pleasure. When given to the Spiritual Eye for its purpose, they become a source of unlearning the ego-thought system that results in peace of mind. Only the Spiritual Eye can make this choice for us, as we offer the little willingness. If moralized religion loses sex as a promoter for guilt and shame, this would be the equivalent of dismantling weapons in a nuclear arsenal. Their war powers have been neutralized. Just remember, sexual urges are really distorted miracle impulses. Give these to the Spiritual Eye, and you will be shown what to do.

The End of Time

Time is a device we have made to separate ourselves from the Love of God. It becomes an instrument for our awakening when given to the Spiritual Eye for His purpose Matthew concludes his teachings of Jesus in the New Testament with the following promise:

"And know that I am with you always; yes, to the end of time."

Those who believe in an inerrant and literal belief of The Book of Revelation speak of "End Times" as if it were a period of years in which horrific events will transpire. The "End Times" phenomenon is a key component in the Myth of the Apocalypse, justified with quotes from the Old and New Testaments. Yet, like *"ACIM'*s" Elder Brother, whom Dr. Schucman felt was Jesus of Nazareth, is speaking of time as a concept in our minds, not a date set in the future. As we discussed earlier, time is subjective. It is fluid for awakening's purposes, not objective as an X on the calendar. The *Manual for Teachers*" suggests time goes backward, in that we can go backward in time to that point where we chose to separate from our Christ identity. This is the moment we have chosen to see ourselves as egos, apart from our God the Father.

In a non-duality philosophy, the world of time is a dream or illusion in our mind. The choice we made to see ourselves as apart from the Christ-Self happens in the world we made. Although this decision was made long ago, it seems to be happening now. What we chose at the beginning of time is given to us again, at each moment in time, to reconsider. We are free to choose, in time, when we will take our curriculum for awakening. While we cannot choose the Course's content itself, we can choose the start time. Realizing our decision to separate can be revisited at any point "in time," we may actually go back to the exact moment we made the choice. This is an instant so ancient it is beyond all memory – even past the possibility of remembering. When we join with our fellow students for a holy purpose, the coming together is always at the right place and the time is right, "in time." The ancient memory becomes the present, and what appears to be a new encounter really happened before time began long beyond our ego's memory. This memory lives outside of time, where we were never really separated.

What will happen when time ends? "ACIM" has an answer. Time seems eternal, but it will have an end. Forgiveness happens "in time."

"Will the stars disappear, and night and day be no more? What will happen to all things that come and go: the tides, the seasons and the lives of man? Will all things that change with time and bloom and fade, will they not return?" ACIM

These are but the images we made to occupy our minds while time waits on timelessness. Timelessness is the absence of time, and not "in time." Where time has set an end is not where the eternal is. These are the measures we have made to count time, yet when time is no more, their purpose for existing will go away. We seek return to the eternal, outside of time, but in reality we never left the eternal. This is the paradox of time: no easy answers and never fully understood. We must employ a thought system outside of time to understand what we have made. Time cannot answer the riddle of timelessness.

The Voice explains: God's Son, the eternal Christ-Self, cannot be changed to something our egos have made. He will be as He was and as He is, for time did not appoint his destiny, nor set the hour of his birth and death. Forgiveness will not change us, yet time waits upon forgiveness, for the things of time will disappear when they have no use. Nothing survives its purpose. If it is conceived to die, then die it must. Otherwise, it must make forgiveness its own purpose. Change is the only thing that can be made a blessing, in time, where purposes are not fixed, however changeless it may appear. We cannot set a goal other than God's purpose for ourselves, and then establish it as changeless and eternal. We cannot give ourselves a purpose we do not have to give. Fortunately, we cannot remove the inherent power to change our minds and use it for any other reason. The power to remember our Christ-Self cannot be changed nor removed. Change is the greatest gift God gave to all. We cannot make change eternal, nor can Heaven pass away. There is no time in Heaven, only timelessness.

The Course's Voice does not tell us we were born to die. We cannot change our eternal being, because our function has been fixed by God. All other goals are set "in time;" with one exception, they will change so time might be preserved. Forgiveness does not aim at keeping time but at its ending, when time has no use. Its purpose ended, it is gone. Where time once seemed to hold sway, it is now restored to the function God established for us in our full awareness. Time can set no end to its fulfillment or its changelessness. There is no death because as eternal beings, we share the function our Creator gave to us. Life's function cannot be to die. It must be life's extension that we are as one forever and forever, without end.

"ACIM" explains this world will bind our feet, tie our hands and kill our bodies only if we think this world was made to crucify us as the living the Son of God. While we may dream of death, it does not need to stand as the purpose of our dream. This is the key to the end of time.

The Rapture: "We Know Not the Time, We Know Not the Place"

Words from an old gospel hymn express uncertainties of "End Times" philosophies. Cultural myths foment fear in our unconscious minds. They cast seeds of outrage, terror and war. No wonder we are plagued with conflict and turmoil, sickness and poverty. In an apocalyptic context, the Rapture is a broadly held belief Jesus of Nazareth will return and, along with a selected few, will be taken bodily back to

Heaven. This event will transpire either prior to the onset or during, a period of tribulation. This depends on your theology. Only the "chosen ones" will avoid the terrible events awaiting those "left behind" on earth. Theories and speculation on time, place and conditions precedent are points of great contention. Individual theologies vary on the application of tribulation or the period between Rapture and the End of Time.

Prophecies of battles between good and evil joined with the angst of the Last Judgment fosters tremendous fear among believers and non-believers. To experience an understanding of this fear, imagine an eternal wait in the dentist office with full access to the sounds, smells and views of a patient getting a root canal – without gas or pain killers for you or the patient. Now cover that terror with layers of denial and stuff it deep down inside, hoping it goes away. This is what our unconscious minds mold: horrific fear. We are in an eternal wait for a final judgment where only 144,000 will be selected from billions for a few good seats. This ratio is not good. There is a reason prisoners of war have difficulty recovering from daily torture; most die rather than endure the pain. There is little chance for reprieve. With a ratio of thousands to billions, hope is faint. We are prisoners in our own camp of fear, waiting punishment without an execution date

There is Another Way.

"ACIM" ask that each of us join in a Great Crusade to reveal Truth. Willingness is our mode of expression, forgiveness the means of awakening our Christ-Self by recognizing this presence in each of our brothers. This is the Rapture's real meaning. It all takes place "in time," the device made by our ego-self to maintain separation. Fortunately, the Spiritual Eye, our communication link with God, transcends our belief that time is real and God Himself awaits our return at the end of time. We are not alone. A friend has come to help. He has walked in the footsteps of this journey. This is the author of "A Course in Miracles" and the internal Teacher. His purpose is to hold our hand while we experience the Rapture, the process of awakening to our Divinity.

"ACIM" redefines the Rapture and other apocalyptic terms as a release, not an entrapment. The Rapture is not a physical event, but a state of awareness we already have in our unconscious mind. It is awaiting recognition. The *"Workbook for Students"* accompanying

"*ACIM*" defines (Daily Lesson No. 151) Rapture as the joy and happiness we will experience when we recognize the Face of Christ; it will happen as we listen to the Voice for God. Rapture is subjective, not objective. The veil metaphor refers to the many objects we make that prevent us from seeing our own Divinity's presence. This is Christ in our fellows as a reflection of our own Christ-Self. We have made many veils. The belief in time which keeps us linear and separated is a dark veil. Worship of material items we can possess or the belief we are bodies – and not spirits – are veils as well. Lists continue, but none of these are the great veil which dims our view. There is one veil darker than others.

Blocking the Face of Christ, Our Dedication to Death

Our greatest obstacle to Peace is a belief that death is real. This obstacle is our darkest veil, hanging before the Face of Christ. This belief is upheld and protected by our actual attraction to death. I only recently understood the concept of being attracted to death. How anyone could be attracted to ending life, with no assurance of a hereafter, was a mystery to me.

"*ACIM*" is vehement that we are dedicated to death. We have made a solemn vow in secret with our egos. This is the darkest shroud, the veil we will never lift nor look upon. We have agreed, with our egos, not to suspect or speculate death even exists. In making this secret bargain, we have forever blotted from our memories what lies beyond the veil. This is our total dissociation from the memory of God; we are in concert with our ego minds. We have made a promise to never consciously join again with our Christ-Self or even to look at the fear which shrouds God's Love.

Let me share a personal reference, my most difficult lessons to understand. When I began this writing, my father was dying of old age and many afflictions. We moved him and my mother 60 miles away from their farm and community to be with my brother in a large city. When I visited to care for them, my anxiety would hang in the air. My father suffered from dementia, my mother from Alzheimer's; both were obsessed with going "home." I responded to my fear of their death with frustration and anger. I remember my selfish thoughts: God, when will this end? God, don't let them die. Many times I felt a quick and sudden death would bring relief, a veiled attraction. Life at this stage has few pretty moments.

144

In a recent visit, my daughter and I had to restrain my father from attempting to walk home. Because of a heart problem and Parkinson's disease, he had lost mobility in his legs. We put him back in his chair, even though he could not walk unaided. How my father escaped broken bones, I will never know. It was a daily humiliation to watch his attempts to walk and then his falls. He would threaten to hit us with his cane for restraining him, but we had to bring the cane first. In the evenings, we would laugh with him at the situation, but at the moment it was a confused mess of emotions. He did not want to use a wheel chair and he did not remember that he couldn't walk – or he chose not to remember.

Seeing him struggle was a threat to my own mortality. I would usually visit every 30 days, noticing the drastic changes in their mental and physical appearances. Death becomes very real when it is defined as deterioration of the body. Mom and Dad's physical and mental condition declined rapidly over the final 90 days.

Fishing for Answers

My father and I were not emotionally close in my childhood. We struggled with the verbal language of expressing love from a father to a son. It was a language I was unable to hear at my young age. Our experiences were shared through activities rather than the intellectual discourse I craved. He was an avid fisherman and together we fished most of the streams within reasonable distance of our farm. We were rewarded whether casting in waders for perch and smallmouth bass in spring-fed Ozark creeks or from boats on lakes for largemouth bass and catfish, always coming home with a mess of fish.

My favorite fishing was spear fishing or "gigging" during winter nights, aided by the light of bright gas mantles on a wooden johnboat. The Gasconade River had its headwaters in our community. It was perfect for paddling up and down stretches of slow-moving water between rapids or riffles. We referred to these expanses as "holes" of water. The larger ones were given specific names such as the Blue, the Sycamore and the Cottonmouth Hole (the least favorite). Cottonmouths are poisonous water snakes, which inhabit fresh water in most southern states. They are known for aggressively pursuing a fisherman's catch, dropping off overhanging tree limbs or crawling up and over the side of a johnboat. At that point, most brave fishermen abandoned ship.

These expanses of water were 6-10 feet deep. The Cottonmouth Hole was bottomless, or so I was told. An appointed fisherman would use a steel, three-point gig at the end of a long pine pole to spear fish on the stream bottoms. During the cold winters, the water was crystal clear and the cottonmouths were in their nests. More than once, the evening fire was used to dry wet clothing, in addition to frying up the night's take. A fireplace and warm feather bed felt wonderful after a night of gigging in ice-cold water.

My father and I were not strangers; we just never shared affection or conversation in the fashion I anticipated. During one "parent sitting" visit, I found Dad hobbling across the floor to get his coat. He was going home. I said, "Dad, you are going to fall and hit your head." Almost immediately, he dropped his cane and fell forward into my arms. As he was falling forward, I faintly heard my name and "cottonmouth" mumbled in the same sentence. I was able to catch his fall and keep him standing.

We stood there ever so long, not saying a word. I held him around his shoulders. Finally, he spoke, saying, "What are we going to do?" I responded, "I suppose I will stand here and hold you until you until you decide to lie back down in bed." After a few more moments of hugging, I helped him back to bed. I am not sure who initiated the move, but I realized an important message. His love was communicated with actions, not words. I just needed ears to hear. Somehow, our closeness and my change in roles from care-taking to care-giving helped me remember the loving moments from my childhood. They had remained unspoken and beyond recall.

A Course to the Rescue

Fortunately, I found a local "*A Course in Miracles*" discussion group in Missouri and started attending after an angry interchange over walking and going home. During this particular session, the group was studying our belief in the "dream of death." The reading turned into a maximal learning experience for me. We discussed this very belief that death is real and that we are attracted to it. In a perverse way, I could understand the attraction. Seeing my parents' daily struggle to function made dying more attractive than this humiliating struggle to stay alive. The thought of personally experiencing this was very unpleasant, even frightening. Aging with grace must be an art.

"*ACIM*'s" solution was to give all my dreams of death to the Spiritual Eye. One interpretation of "*ACIM*" metaphysics would be that anything outside Heaven's realm is not real and therefore, a dream. We have either waking dreams or sleeping dreams. This is the philosophy of non-duality. As we discussed earlier,"*ACIM*" proposes a non-dualistic context whereby there is no Heaven or parallel world here on Earth; there is only a Heaven in which we reside as the Christ-Self. What remains outside of Heaven as our mind and body is not seen in the Eyes of God. The world we experience is of our own making and not real to God. Some would define this as a world of illusions, not reality. The "real world" in "*ACIM*'s" context is only in Heaven. "Real world" is a phrase unique to "*ACIM*" with its own special meaning. This philosophy works well in the class room or discussion group, but not so well when giving personal care to a dying parent.

In reality, our conscious experiences are dreams of separation from Heaven. One of "*ACIM*'s" purposes s to awaken us from this dream. As long as I am defining death as a wasting body, then death is very real. In a world of non-duality where only spirit is real, a deteriorating body is not reality, but my belief in a waking dream of sickness and death. If we believe death is part of the waking dream, our bodies are real. We do not remember we are spirits. Another function of the Spiritual Eye is to give new meaning to our dreams; He will use them for his Truth and healing purposes. This reference is for both sleeping dreams and waking dreams.

As we began to discuss this "*ACIM*" concept in our study group that night in Missouri, the source of anger at my father became apparent to me. His deterioration was making the dream of death real. I was angry at him for what I had chosen in my own mind. When I returned home that night, my father was in the wheel chair and our anger had subsided. I know intellectually fear arises when we begin to look at the greatest obstacle to peace, the attraction of death and the fear of accepting our true identity as the Christ. We are eternal beings who were never born and will never die. This may be what Jesus referred to when he spoke of being in this world, but not of this world. Holding this idea intellectually while being invested in the dream of death emotionally is a sure road to the insane asylum. Unfortunately, letting go of our belief in the dream of death appears to be the precursor to the end of time. This is the reason it is our last and most difficult lesson.

I have often questioned why my parents clung to life so insistently, as their daily effort to function was exhausting to watch, let alone experience. We sat together in silence many times. I would catch Dad from the corner of his eye looking at me. For an instant, I realized that his mind is all knowledge and awareness of a fully evolved spiritual teacher. Their Spirits was never born, and therefore never died. They are the Christ-Self, eternal and beyond time.

My parents passed away 30 days apart from each other. They had been together for more than 60 years and I am convinced that each was waiting for the other to go first. In retrospect, our emotional closeness that developed in the last year was worth every sleepless night and uncomfortable moment. I have only fond memories remaining in my mind of my time with them as a child, as well as the final months before they passed away.

Teach Them Well for They Have Chosen You

Our two children were baptized in Unity Village near Kansas City, Missouri. I distinctly remember the Unity Ministers as they read from the liturgy's baptismal service. They presented a concept that was quite disturbing to me at the time with their affirmation to us as parents: "You should always remember, you are not the parents of these children, you are their teachers. Teach them well, for they have chosen you!" This was a difficult concept to grasp, that we have been chosen by our children as their teachers. If this were true, our life pre-existed birth and unborn spirits have the intelligence to pick their parents so as to teach them lessons in this life time.

If it were true for my children, then it is true for me also. Had I chosen my parents? If so, among the many lessons I had selected my parents to teach – the attraction to and fear of death – was the greatest and must have been on my lesson plan. It is also the most difficult lesson as I continue to learn. Our Spirit never dies; death is not real. Only deterioration of the body is real. I am thankful for the pleasant memories I keep of their lives. As we sat in silence over those last few months, I awakened to a new reality. I had chosen the perfect parents. They were excellent teachers, for they taught the lesson for which I was seeking:

"This is our Son in whom we are well pleased."

The Apocalypse as Final Lifting of the Veil

The Greek word apokalypsis means "the lifting of a veil," or uncovering something that has been hidden. This reference to lifting the veil is consistently used in "*ACIM*" as a metaphor for the sudden awareness of knowledge and as an explanation of Revelation. As you will recall, Revelation comes directly from God. The Course's Voice can indirectly inspire Revelation because he is ever listening for those who are Revelation-ready. In our methods of upside-down thinking, the Apocalypse has taken on a meaning of endless battles with fear and uncertainty about our future. It manifests itself in the plagues, famine and conflict we fight daily. So great is this fear we can't even recall the original meaning of the word. We are terrified and afraid to look at our mistake.

The only way we can look upon this terror is to hold the hand of our brothers and look together. The Course's Voice asks that we respond to him as if he were an Elder Brother, giving respect because of his experience and because he has gone before us to make our way easier. We must assume he has looked upon this fear, seen its nothingness, recognized the Face of Christ and accepted the Love of God for himself. He makes his experience available to us and will hold our hand as we awaken gently to the awareness of God's presence.

Each of us has a hidden desire to see the Face of Christ. This is the motivating principle in our life, underlying layers of denial and our belief in separation. It presents itself in symbols of symbols that the ego continuously misrepresents. Unfortunately, the fear of this realization has taken on apocalyptic proportions. It becomes insurmountable to do by ourselves. We must hold the hands of our brothers.

The next chapter contains guidelines on how to form a study group and suggestions on reading "*ACIM*" in a manner to foster awareness or awakening to this inner reality. Beginning the process does have its perils. Be aware of the seven-head monster that will raise his head and say, "Do not look here." Rest assured, only the "little willingness" needs be offered to the Spiritual Eye, and relief will come.

This "looking" process is the true meaning of Apocalypse, the lifting of the veil. Setting our thinking "right" is the process of gently awakening. This will bring about a change in perception in how we view life. We are awakening from a dream of fear. *"ACIM"* refers to what we will experience as the "Happy Dream". Our apocalyptic fear of awakening will speed by with the force of a high speed train. Without tribulation, these fears will look like nothing more than a thin black line.

Now... Lifting of the Veil

We have spoken much about miracles. Revelation comes directly from God and functions outside of time and space. You may think of this in terms of a vertical axis. It proceeds directly from God to us. Miracles, on the other hand, are a change in our perception. They suspend time and should be thought of in a horizontal axis, affecting relationships between us and our fellows. Miracles suspend time for only an instant and at that moment, we correct our Vision. The Course's Voice is in charge of miracles and will direct each of us to perform our assigned miracles throughout the day, when we ask and listen. With continued study, a new understanding of miracles will follow as will their application on an experiential level.

Miracles, or the holy instant, are what we experience by "lifting of the veil" that has been drawn across the Face of Christ in our brother. While we stand in seeming terror, the Course's Voice will hold our hand as will the Elder Brother, whom a loving Father has entrusted with our care. We will learn to see beyond the things we have made. Our ego sees these fears as a supposed friend because they protect us from the Love of God. Once the veil is lifted, we will see the insanity of our love of sin and the separation from God. The appeal of guilt that buffers us from our brothers will begin to lose its hold.

Our fear of the ego's vengeance, our praise for death, will vanish before our eyes; these are also our friend. They are our protectors we have made to vouchsafe our brother's identity. Like sunshine on a mirror, the radiance and warmth of his reality will reflect on our face, erasing any shadows of doubt or tribulation. We will know whose hand we hold and what path we travel. We have assigned fear of abandonment as our on punishment for looking at the protectors of the veil. It will leave us and the awareness of what attracts us to our brothers – the Face of Christ beyond the veil – will become obvious.

The Holy Instant, a glimpse beyond the veil, will only last for a moment. Time collapses in this instant, saving thousands of years.

Our Guide, the Course's Voice, is ever ready to stand with us when we undertake this task. This is offering our "little willingness" to look, once again, beyond the veil of time we have made. We have made the friend and protectors of the ego: fear, guilt and death. They will disappear. We only need to accept the Atonement for ourselves. We will become willing to see our brothers differently, looking beyond the images we made in our minds. In this act of forgiveness, we are saved forever. This is baptism in the Spirit, washed clean of our sin of denial and our belief in separation.

Our journey now takes on new purpose. Having been to the mountaintop and having seen beyond the terror we have made, we have been Transfigured. The guilty images of the past and fearful visions of the future are seen in true perspective through the Vision of the Spiritual Eye. We are no longer held hostage to the dark shadows of our past or the four horsemen of the future. Our journey has begun, not come to an end. But there is more work to be done. We have more tasks to perform.

Sue and Labor on His Behalf

I want to use an analogy to make a point. Having worked with insurance companies for many years, I have always been captivated by the wording of Lloyd's of London ocean marine policy. It enumerates duties and obligations of policyholders in the event of insurance losses. The "Sue and Labor" clause is one of my favorites. It defines the responsibilities of the insured to preserve, protect and salvage the remains of any vessel and cargo following a disaster. It is not just a request, it is an obligation to "sue and labor" on behalf of the underwriters to mitigate the loss. This would include recovering cargo and salvaging the vessel, if at all possible.

Imagine, if you will, that we have made a disaster of thought in our own minds. We have wrecked a beautiful vessel created by God. The salvage operation must begin and we must act. We shall undertake to "sue and labor" on his behalf for recovery of any salvageable wreckage and protect the undamaged cargo by any reasonable means. Let me use another insurance term with an appropriate analogy. Agents are the independent sales force of the industry. Before modern communications, agents were representatives of the insurance company and not necessarily employees. Given that ocean voyages could take months and claims had to be paid, agents were given express authority to act on behalf of the insurance companies to fulfill the contract's obligations. This is called a principle-agency relationship. It is a relationship of "utmost good faith." The agent must act in the best interest and on behalf of the principal, knowing in complete confidence the principal will support his every effort without fail. As the relationship is built on faith and trust, it is of the highest order, based on mutual interest and goodwill.

Let's continue the analogy. We have such a relationship with the Guide, author and Voice of the Course. A disaster of apocalyptic proportions is in the making. We have an obligation to "sue and labor" on His behalf, knowing full well that as our Principle, He will support every effort with "utmost good faith." These are reassuring words. As we accept the Atonement for ourselves, a glimpse beyond the veil will be given us. Our obligation to "sue and labor" will become a source of peace and happiness, not arduous servitude. Clear the wreckage from your mind. The salvage operation must begin within us. We may undertake this work knowing full well we act in "utmost good faith" and will receive our Principle's unending grace. He will support our every effort as we accept our function in this Plan of At-one-ment. Our salvage operation, otherwise known as our salvation, begins today.

God's Plan of Salvation

The Course's Voice is responsible for this Salvage Plan, or God's Plan of Salvation. He will assign miracles to perform each day for those ready to offer their "little willingness." We need not look far to see applications. Each of us stands next to someone who will offer the chalice of Atonement, for the Spiritual Eye is within him as well. Will I choose to see him sinless with Vision from the Spiritual Eye, or will I hold his sins against him? The one beside me brings the gift of salvation and when I accept this gift of forgiveness, he has the power to clear this wreckage from my mind. Do I call my giver of salvation friend or enemy? Offering this gift to him means I will receive it for myself. This is the choice in my mind. We need each other; I cannot offer forgiveness to myself nor can he give it to himself alone. Our Savior stands beside us awaiting our call to awaken. We will both be reborn. If I chose to see him any other way, I have chosen to turn Love into an enemy. This cannot be.

If you are as skeptical as I am, please realize the Spiritual Eye will use time on his behalf. Over time, a comfortable relationship evolves with these terms and the concepts behind them. How do I relate to a Voice which dictates to me and others? How would I respond to an awareness or understanding of a direct communication link with the Divine? A relationship of "utmost good faith" is something that evolves into trust and understanding through trial and error. Over time, we begin to "know" this is real. It comes quickly for some, slower for others. Fortunately, time is under our control.

But time is of the essence. We must not linger. Waste no time with indecision, for we have miracles to perform. Waste no time with uncertainty, for the End of Time, as we know it, is drawing near.

The Tribulation

In the traditional myth of the Apocalypse, the Tribulation is a period of upheaval. This is usually seven years in length, during which the Devil will exert control over the earth through the antichrist. All but a small remnant of the Christian faithful will perish. No more than 144,000 will remain. Everyone else will die as a result of wars, plagues and famine. The Tribulation will end with Christ's defeat of the antichrist at Armageddon before he establishes God's millennial kingdom on earth. Again, Christ is personalized in the Myth as an individual, not the enlightened thought of God in our minds. He is returning as a military leader, just as pre-Christian Jews believed prior to the birth of Jesus of Nazareth.

As metaphor, the Devil is our ego and has united with our self-images as bodies, the "real" antichrist, to exert control over our earth. We, too, look amiss. We are in tribulation! At every moment, in time, when we decide our true reality is our body controlled by our ego, we have chosen with the antichrist.

"*ACIM*" indicates the Myth of Tribulation need not be, for it is not true in the world. The Course's Voice has already overcome tribulation for us and will show how we can do the same. This would be the period of study required by each individual until the Christ awakens in conscious memory, the Second Coming into our mind. The millennial kingdom is the waiting period in which we are now engaged. This is our holding position, when we perform miracles awaiting a sufficient number to awaken and initiate this "Speed-Up."

Only 144,000 will remain. Numbers are symbols too; this number is the symbol of wholeness. When the Book of Revelation was written, the number of Christians was quiet small, so 144,000 would have appeared to be a large sum. It is the square of 12 times 1,000. As Dr. Edinger has noted, this is the symbol of completeness. It is one, the collective Christ already in our minds and the living memory of God that has never left our thoughts. This is knowledge awaiting our reconnection. We need not suffer nor endure misery while in tribulation, waiting for a sufficient number to awaken. Our suffering has been accomplished for us.

"*ACIM's*" author suggests we undertake to learn this lesson together so we can be free of our tribulations together. He needs devoted teachers who share his aim to heal the mind. We are far beyond the need of protection. He asks us to remember this:

> "*In this world you NEED not have tribulation BECAUSE I have overcome the world. THAT is why you should be of good cheer.*" "*ACIM.*"

The "Celestial Speed-Up" is accelerating us through this period of tribulation. In the vast expanse of time, which we believe is real, we are but a few milliseconds away from the Great Awakening. This is a truth about time and tribulation.

Chapter 7

The Seven Headed Beast,

Symbol of Completion

Seven Horns,

Seven Angels,

Seven Churches,

Seven Eyes on the Lamb

Seven Lamps before the Throne,

Seven Stars in the hand of Christ,

Seven Seals fastening a Scroll....

.........and the seventh seal shall lead to seven trumpets. And these trumpets will herald the coming of a great message, for you now have ears to hear. What is the message of seven? It must be extremely important to be smitten so repeatedly. Numbers are symbols and as such, the number 7 is an outer image of a powerful archetype now coming into our conscious awareness. It is the symbol of the "Archetype of the Apocalypse" that precedes the coming of the individuated Christ-Self, our personal Second Coming.

The number 3 is an ancient symbol of becoming. It is masculine in nature. It foretells the approach of something great, but not complete. Christianity is a religion of threes. There were three wise men coming to visit the Christ Child. There were three at the Transfiguration, accompanied by three Disciples; only with the Holy Spirit did Transfiguration come into fruition. There were three in the lions' den. Job's three friends came to ease his suffering. The Holy Trinity speaks for itself. There were three on the cross. The cross itself is distorted. It lacks symmetry and begs for completeness, with one arm extending downward. Three is a symbol of becoming. It suffers the pain of birth and the agony of death. It can bear nothing else but a crown of thorns.

Western society lives in a three-dimensional world. This is the world of matter and senses; it perceives nothing but the literal. Only scientific proof is valid in this world – the unseen, the unproven, the unknown are pushed aside as fantasy and laughable. Mystery, awe and inspiration have no value. Listen to the debate surrounding the creation story and how it will be taught in our public schools. In one corner is the scientist with proof from the laboratory. In the other corner are the creationists with their literal account of seven days. Myth's mystery has no standing to sue in this proceeding. William Jennings Bryan put literalism on trial against science during the historic State of Tennessee vs. Scopes trial. Fact, proof, testimony and justice do not touch the realm of Spirit. The beliefs of Western fundamentalist religions do not ask for belief in the unseen, but demand belief in the unreasonable. It knows nothing of the Spirit that resides in the fourth dimension. Trinity is masculine; it craves union with the feminine, nurturing Spirit. It lacks unconditional forgiveness offered by the more feminine forgiving intuition, so necessary to enter the fourth realm.

Four: The Symbol of Completeness

The archetype of four is a symbol of completeness. If three is the process, four is the end result. It lacks nothing; it is fulfillment. Adding 1 to 3 does not make 4; it lives in another realm, far beyond fact or scientific proof. Four is like the crosshairs in a telescope; it brings focus, acuity and vision. Primitive and Eastern religions use symbols of wholeness revealed as 4: the four winds, the four seasons. Their circles are mandalas, or images of completion.

The archetype of four finds its source of strength comes from the spheres in the heavens. Circles are a mandala of wholeness, such as images of the Moon and the Sun. Visit the Catholic Church at the Taos Reservation in New Mexico or any South American country, and you will see the Virgin Mary's prominence among their icons. She has her place of equality with the Father, the Son and Holy Ghost. These congregations are maternal. The Virgin Mary represents completeness. She is the mother, full, supple and inclusive. Quaternity is union of the opposites. It is comfortable with both the masculine and the feminine. When united, they create the holy union

156

and deliver the Christ Child into our minds as the fruit of their mystical marriage.

Consider the ancient Celtic cross, a symbol of successors to the English druids. The arms of their cross are symmetrical, covered by a circle. It is not distorted nor preoccupied with suffering, death and agony. This cross was not designed for cruci-fiction. Its mission was to feed and care for the community through its ministry. It is concerned less about proving its theology with legalistic views. These are symbols of wholeness. They are not distorted with messages of fear, condemnation or moral turpitude.

Seven as the Process of Awakening

Seven is 3 next to 4. It is the symbol of awakening, the archetype of process, individuation and completeness. It symbolizes change and transformation. It is the outward symbol of the "Archetype of the Apocalypse." To enter the realm of the Spirit, one must leave our world of the known; the certain and the literal must be abandoned. It is easier for a camel to enter the eye of a needle than for the rich man to enter the world of Spirit. Lip service will not suffice. Transformation upsets our world. All that we value is no longer dependable; it must be released.

Job found relief when his fourth friend came to offer repentance. Dr. Edinger suggests when confronted with 3, it is proper to ask, "Where is 4?" Is it equally proper when confronted with 4 to ask, "Where is 3?" The 12 steps of addiction recovery are three sets of four or four sets of three. All 12 disciples were given a message of completeness. Seven is the sum of 4 and 3. They are not melded together, but a synthesis is required. This is the mystery of the Book of Revelation and why the Apocalypse is so frightening. It is our egos' foot servant; it says, "Do not look beyond here or you will perish in eternal damnation."

Jung suggested individuation is a continuing process, like the ebb and flow of a mountain spring. We reach fulfillment only to be confronted with the proposition of becoming all over again. This is an ever-continuing spiral always returning upward to the beginning for more unlearning, then more awakening. It will continue until all awaken. This is life initiating itself at the urge for renewal.

Drugs and alcohol will not kill the pain that shrouds our craving for the emerging spirit. Guns cannot protect us from our fear of the Second Coming. Death is not an escape, but only a delay. We must be Transfigured. This is the individuation process that Jesus of Nazareth undertook as symbolized by the crucifixion. He died to his sense of ego-self and awakened to his Christ-Self. He understood the unreality of death through resurrection. What died was His belief in separation. This is the sin for which He saved our lives: the agony of tribulation and the belief in separation. We need not suffer in this world, because He suffered for us. Buddha suggested we participate joyously in the world's suffering. Both Buddha and Jesus of Nazareth rose above the pain of suffering, but they remained to comfort and teach us. Their spirits are the internal Teachers in our mind.

Fear says do not undertake this journey or enter on the pathway of unlearning. Fortunately, we have many Teachers who have gone before us. They know the way. One is the Voice of the Course, who has been with us always. He is in charge of our transformation plan and will deliver us from this attraction to death and our nightmares. He will teach us to perform miracles and offer the gift of forgiveness; this is our pathway to freedom. We need offer only a little willingness.

Unfortunately, there are times when even this "little willingness" seems beyond memory and exceeds our grasp. We are so firmly entrenched in our three-dimensional world we cannot recall the thought of something beyond. It is the mental state that Socrates referred to when describing generals, "They do not know that they do not know."

If you listen to the personal accounts of recovery in the many 12-step programs, a consistent common theme evolves irrespective of addiction or geographic location. These stories generally terminate in a state of near death or suicide. All other remedies have been exhausted and the suffering Soul describes a sense of acute anxiety and desperation. Having no other options, they reach out to some unknown source asking for help, rather than to die. The next step usually tells of an intervention, arrest, an unsolicited call or decision to seek help which leads them to a 12-step meeting and subsequent recovery. Something of the unknown or in the unseen is able to penetrate the mental fog of addiction and responds to the call for help. It bridges the gap between the ego-ruled world of three dimensions.

The Soul awakens from this perspective into the fourth dimension, being rocketed into another realm. Who is this unseen matchmaker that pierces the fog of addiction? What is its name and how does it work? I suggest it is the Course's Voice performing modern-day miracles. This is the savior bridging the tiny gap by extending his hand as a gift of forgiveness. This is not a reprieve but an enlightened mind who knows a sufferer's true identities. This is the Elder Brother of "*ACIM*" seeking to help us along the way.

Our Elder Brother and the Dream of Death

Miracles are the pathway to wholeness, functioning in the three-dimensional world of our perceptions. Miracles suspend time on the horizontal plane. Awe is an inappropriate response to miracles. Unlike miracles, Revelation is literally unspeakable because it is an experience of unspeakable love. Awe should be reserved for Revelation, as it is perfect and correct for this application. It is not appropriate for miracles because a state of awe is one of worship. It implies that one of a lesser order stands before a greater one. This is the case when we stand before our Creator. As spiritual beings, we are perfect creations and experience awe only in the presence of the Creator of perfection. Revelation is the expression of 4; this is Quaternity. If miracles are the process of becoming, Revelation is the state of being complete, a symbol of the Christ-Self. Although individuation is never complete, each temporary state of wholeness must be submitted to the Trinity's dialectic for life to continue. This is the death and rebirth cycle.

"*ACIM*" tell us from the very beginning the miracle is a sign of love among equals. Equals cannot be in awe of one another because awe implies inequality. It is therefore an inappropriate reaction to our Elder Brother, the Course's Voice. An elder brother is entitled to respect for his greater experience and a reasonable amount of obedience for his greater wisdom. He is also entitled to love, because he is a brother, and to our devotion, because he is equally devoted to us. It is this devotion of our Elder Brother that entitles us to his. Our Elder Brother cannot accomplish anything that we can't. The only difference between us and our Elder Brother is that he has nothing that does not come from God. He remains in a state of true holiness that is still only a potential in us. He has risen and no longer needs a body.

The Elder Brother, as the Course's Voice, identifies himself as having the same mind as Christ Jesus, and is therefore familiar with quotes attributed to the Bible's Jesus. Once again, he offers a correction to explain his ability to help us in those times of need when we are only able to offer the "little willingness." For example, the Course's author explains:

"No man cometh unto the Father but by me."

The author indicates this is among the Bible's most misunderstood statements. *"ACIM"* explains it doesn't mean our Elder Brother is in any way separate or different from us, except in time – and time is a creation of our own minds. Actually, the quotation is more meaningful if it is considered on a vertical axis, rather than the horizontal. On this plane, we stand below the Elder Brother and He stands below God. In the process of "rising up," He is higher than we. Without Him, the distance between God and man would be too great for us to transcend.

The Voice likens himself (Miracle Principle No. 50) to an Elder Brother with greater experience and due greater respect from us, along with a reasonable amount of obedience for his wisdom. I had a problem with this idea. My personal experience became a demonstration of how such a difficult relationship, when given to the Spiritual Eye, will be healed.

Healing With the Elder Brother

My brother is five years older than me. We are different in many ways. He is gifted in working with his hands, in his relationships with friends and is a devoted employee, husband and father. We grew up with an intense sibling rivalry that kept us mentally separated from my first memories. The details are really unimportant here. It needs no explanation for those who have experienced this sense of separation.

After studying this Text for a few years, I became aware of the importance of this relationship and how I was avoiding offering an olive branch to mend the fence of separation. Frankly speaking, I had rather enjoyed an inflated sense of accomplishments over the years. I finally began to deal with my "unwillingness" to offer this relationship to the Spiritual Eye in my *"ACIM"* discussion small group. I was in denial about my "unwillingness" and not allowing the relationship to be healed. My inflated ego gave a message of false assurance, hiding behind a veil of smug self importance.

Fortunately we discussed this issue in the "*ACIM*" small group. Others members shared their experiences. By the end of the session, I had mustered the little willingness and offered this relationship to the Spiritual Eye. When we do this, He joins our little willingness with His complete willingness; this union becomes the general goal of Truth and one of the requirements for change from a special relationship to a holy relationship. This change didn't happen overnight or without some duress. It seldom does. The Spiritual Eye's specific instructions are to give Him the "little willingness," and do nothing more. Otherwise, we only waste time by interfering. Beyond that point, we delay the healing. I was happy to oblige.

My older brother and I were forced to work together as our parents aged and died. We developed a friendship that had not existed for many years, though strain still pulls at the bonds. We were able to work together during this two-year period and accomplish what neither of us could have done by ourselves. My troubled relationship with my older brother was a projection of the shrouded relationship with the Course's Elder Brother, my Teacher and Savior. This is the One who would lead me through the process of awakening to the Christ within myself and within others. Until I became willing to heal the relationship with my sibling, I was reluctant to call upon the Teacher inside – the very purpose of "*A Course in Miracles*". My relationship with the Elder Brother, the internal teacher, remained blocked.

As I became aware of the impasse, the willingness to heal the relationship became easier. With the decline in our parents' health bringing about a renewed urgency, we were forced to cooperate. It worked in concert, far beyond what I could have imagined. This was truly a miracle in our family's life.

Overcoming the Fear of the Apocalypse

If we are ever to overcome our fears associated with the Apocalypse and the End Times Myths, we must begin to look at what resides in our minds beyond the grasp of our conscious awareness. This message offers a new way to look at these misunderstandings generated by the Book of Revelation and how the fear of them blocks our awakening. Not everyone needs to do this; only a few need undertake the inner work of seeking a new awareness. Studying in small groups is one of the safest and most effective ways to resolve our individual fears. Everyone has a part to play in God's Plan of Salvation: reading the Text, completing the 365 daily lessons and learning to work miracles. As each of us assume our part, the quickening in the Spirit will begin. If you feel so moved to function as a facilitator of small group study, it is my belief this is an important part in the Plan of Salvation. What follows are guidelines on how to organize and facilitate such groups.

Reading "*A Course in Miracles*"

Abraham Lincoln did not go to law school; he *read* the law. This was the legal profession's accepted method of study well into the 20th Century. While Honest Abe read alone, a more common practice was to study under the guidance of a practicing attorney or judge. A student would prepare for the bar exam through a free flow of questions and answers and an exposure to the legal practice. This is a tried and proven method of learning.

Reading in a group has multiple effects, which become collective. "Reading" under the guidance of a learned instructor is your introduction to "*A Course in Miracles*." This is an effective means of unlearning our ego's thought system. We will literally hold the hand of fellow students as we look upon the fear of the Love of God. The experienced teacher is not an external teacher in the traditional form of an instructor, but The Teacher in your mind who already has all knowledge. This is the same Teacher in the mind of your fellow students. The Teacher's name can be selected individually or by the study group. "*ACIM*" uses many names as well: Friend, Spiritual Eye, Elder Brother, Holy Spirit, Christ, Guide, Comforter and Advisor. You will find many others. We will continue to use different names until the many are one.

Our resistance to unlearning is tremendous. We cannot do it alone. The power of the collective consciousness, when united for a common spiritual purpose, has no opposition. Truth and love will flow like a wellspring, pouring unabated through our minds. Healings' effects are miraculous, blessing both giver and receiver. Rising above time and space as brothers in the collective, we are of the same Christ-Self.

"*ACIM*" suggests over and again that our fellows on this path are the key to our own salvation. Our brother is our Savior, standing beside us as we accept our place in God's Plan of Atonement. Many welcome an opportunity in group study to read aloud, share and discuss. When properly facilitated, a small group will accomplish miracles in unlearning.

Facilitating a Circle of Forgiveness

"Then I heard the voice of the Lord saying:

'Whom shall I send?

Who will be our messenger?' I answered,

'Here I am Lord, send me.' "

Isaiah 6: 8-9.

Those who have decided to accept their place in God's Plan of Atonement may be asked to function by facilitating a "Circle of Forgiveness." I want to offer suggestions based on 10 years of experience. At a minimum, certain things will be required and some situations should be avoided. Study groups are like water; they will find their own level.

I suggest you find a meeting space in an independent location. Many groups meet in homes but if you open a class to public listings for times and places, it becomes difficult to have your home address listed on web sites or published in newsletters. Therefore, you may want to conduct your group in a church, library or other public building (the same suggestions apply to home study groups). A home does offer an intimate setting and calm atmosphere for exchanging ideas. Of course, cancelations, vacations and illnesses can create problems for home groups, so keep this in mind during planning.

Weekly two-hour sessions work best. It can take 30 minutes for everyone to visit, get settled and open the Text to the right place. You will need chairs and the privacy of a room. Some students like to bring reference materials and highlight their Text, so a working surface is desirable. However, arranging tables for 24 can be difficult unless you are in a regular classroom settling. In this situation, a circle works well.

I believe a facilitator is more important to the group than a lecturer or teacher. Facilitators start and stop the discussion, direct the topic and perhaps, through a Socratic method, encourage students to question and participate in the reading and discussion. I have found questions prompted by reading "*A Course in Miracles*" will rise quickly from the group's unconscious without the external focus on a lecturer. The Teacher you want to engage is the internal Teacher and "*ACIM's*" Author.

Finding the Internal Teacher

It is important you face each other to promote a forum for learning experience. This is a process of walking hand-in-hand with your fellow students. Here, no one has greater knowledge or experience than anyone else. The sole purpose of unlearning is the Holy Instant which is directed by our internal Teacher. Again, you will need a facilitator to arrange the setting, moderate the discussion and direct the reading. Hopefully, this will be you.

Many churches do not allow "*ACIM*" classes, as they believe they conflict with their own theology. Public libraries, local schools and even some hospitals have meeting rooms that can be scheduled for a few hours on a predictable basis. Most facilities are open to weekly Twelve-Step meetings, and "*ACIM*" classes are very similar.

I have been with groups that used Al-Anon facilities, which are not bound by AA's traditions or prohibit affiliations with outside groups. Al-Anon sometimes has meeting facilities with tables and chairs, and welcomes donations to help with the rent. Al-Anon rooms may be vacant on Sunday mornings, should you choose to study rather than attend a traditional service. Many Unity churches and some Unitarian Universalist churches see no conflict with "*ACIM*" and allow study groups. I suggest you pay rent for the space with a small contribution, collected weekly. You might establish a prudent reserve for 3-6 months of rent.

Ideally, it is best to avoid amenities that require money. This only creates problems and distracts from your primary purpose. You might want to keep bottled water, tea and coffee on hand. Some groups keep books for sales, if they have the storage space. Keep it simple, for you will begin for a reason – and end just as abruptly.

Storming, Forming, Norming and Performing

I first studied "*A Course in Miracles*" at a small Unity Church in Dallas. The group was comprised of members meeting weekly for two hours. Very few in our group were familiar with the Text or its terms. A smaller number had attempted individual lessons in the original workbook. About 30 attended during the first month; we sat helter-skelter with our facilitator riding roughshod over the discussion. There were arguments, raised voices and just good general chaos. Some members became so frustrated they just walked out. Like all new groups, we were experiencing the process of acclimation: storming, forming, norming and performing.

This free-for-all continued for several months while we collectively groped, then grouped for patterns, procedures and methods. The disorder was our ego's reaction to the prospect of choosing differently, which can be frightening. The chaos and arguments within the group were reflective of the fear and confusion experienced in our own minds. This is our ego's response to our individual and collective questioning of its lack of wisdom. Fortunately, when two or more come together for a spiritual purpose, the Spiritual Eye is there as well. This brings true vision and always corrects our misperceptions. Such was our personal experience.

Chaos: And It Came to Pass...It Didn't Come To Stay

Out of this chaos and confusion evolved a phenomenal pattern I see frequently in study groups committed to reading "*ACIM*." Remember, words are but symbols of symbols, twice removed from reality. They reflect meaning in our unconscious mind. Our ego appears to speak first and speak loudest. Choosing with the ego will only bring unhappiness, depression and despair. Even at its very best it can only produce hatred.

When we offer words or symbols of symbols up to our internal Guide or Spiritual Eye, we receive corrected perception. Then – and only then – will we see beyond blocks preventing peace of mind and peace within the group. Images of our fellows as the bodies they inhabit are the blocks that restrict a flow of forgiveness into conscious awareness. The Spiritual Eye – the Voice for God – is calm, ready and alert to the miracle-minded and will join with us when we set Truth as a goal. He takes our "little willingness" and unites it with His general goal of

Truth. This is where miracles begin to flow: over, around and through these obstructions to peace of mind from the Love of God. It is as if they were washed away. This was our group's experience.

Our numbers were reduced to around 20 regular members when the church relocated to new facilities and our original leader moved to a far country (West Texas). Our new space was in a Unity Church facility's library, formally a post office. We sat in a circle without a second row in our new configuration, making space for newcomers by simply expanding our Circle. Our new facilitator was a wonderful lady named Judy, a counselor at a local high school. She served as our group leader for the next 10 years. Week after week, we came to the Circle and read the Course.

The Answer is in the Next Paragraph

Our weekly patterns involved first welcoming each other, and then praying to invite the Spiritual Eye (or Holy Spirit) to guide our minds, hearts and vision. Opening our books, we began reading the "*ACIM*" Text, one paragraph at a time. As group members became more comfortable over the months, I noticed we shared more personal experiences. The resulting discussions developed into questions about the paragraph we were reading. It was as if the words (symbols of symbols) were prompting questions from the group, questions that were shared in all minds. We became less reluctant to share and more familiar with each other, expanding on the questions as they evolved.

Sometimes, these discussions became unyielding and turned into arguments, complaint sessions, never-ending recitals and other useless diatribes. Fortunately, Judy had the patience of Job. She allowed us to ramble until we had reached the ridiculous, at which point someone would suggest we return to the Text and continue reading. Inevitably, we would find an answer to our questions in the next paragraph. At first, we thought it only coincidental and humorous. Then, ever so slowly, we as a group begin to realize very specific answers to our questions would always follow in the next paragraph.

These answers were related to *"ACIM"* and the lesson it was teaching for that particular section. We did not get answers to objective queries. Our questions usually developed from disagreements in content or over a paradox we could not agree to. When it became apparent there was "no clear answer," someone would suggest we read the next paragraph. Within a few minutes, the answers usually came forth into our conscious awareness, with instructions or suggestions to find a solution. It always worked.

As I attended other groups, I noticed questions arose in the same manner from the paragraphs we read. I found it interesting to watch someone in the group attempt to lecture or redirect the reading to another part of the Text in a circuitous route. Eventually, someone else would suggest they could find an answer in the next paragraph. There would be laughter at the simplicity of the solution, and then someone would begin reading. Calm descended over the group as the answers emerged from the reading. It is amazing to see the pattern of questions and answers working in concert with the Author's ingenuity. Well, it's a miracle.

Begin at the Beginning

Our Unity Church group found it best to begin at the beginning of the Introduction. When we were finished with the Text, we would complete the workbook's lessons, *"The Manual for Teachers* and with terms and definitions which follow or the *"Song of Prayer"* pamphlet (it can take up to a year to complete the material). Some of the book's sections coincide with Christian holidays such as Easter and Christmas, and we would skip to those sections during that time before resuming our routine. We found it important to maintain a rhythm of reading, discussion, clarifying the arising questions and then reading the next paragraph or two until we satisfied the questions in our minds. No sooner did we receive an answer than the next question would emerge from the discussion. A customized lesson plan evolved of unlearning the ego thought system, tailored specifically to the members present.

We are being called together as groups for a purpose. The sooner we can acknowledge our purpose, the sooner we will enjoy peace of mind and happiness. One purpose is to unlearn our faulty ego thought system," and it is amazing how this works. At Unity Church, our rhythm would be off at times or we would be focused on distractions.

But year in and year out, the pattern of reading continuing, page by page, and then moving on to the next paragraph. Reading calmed troubled souls like water on parched lips. It really worked.

A group should be prepared for certain distractions. Some students want to become lecturers and teach, but our function is to learn as one among equals. In fact, we have already accepted our function at a deep unconscious level; we need only bring it into conscious awareness and make it the focal point of our existence. In reality, we should say it "is" the focal point of our existence.

Be aware of temptations to jump around in the Text. When redirecting the focus to another paragraph out of the reading sequence, we break the pattern of questioning and answering inherent in the readings. You may want to explain your reading method at the beginning of the class for this very reason. Jumping from chapter to chapter will break the unlearning process. This work's focus is to encourage small groups to begin looking at our minds' ego myths that create chaos in our world. This is our inner work. It needs an inner Teacher.

A Vigilante for the Holy Spirit

One "*ACIM*" section calls for awareness of the Holy Spirit; this is your call. Be vigilant to the unlearning process. Obviously, there are many ways to conduct the study group, but I have seen this pattern work. It will keep the group focused on the agenda, and you won't have to spend your time as a debate coach. External teachers are a projection of our own minds. They become a real challenge for facilitators and fellow students who have experienced the internal Teacher's ingenuity. Learning to reconcile the group's "unlearning" experience with an external teacher spending time turning pages to prove a point will become a challenge you will learn to harness.

When a guest lecturer must assume the role of one among equals, they usually leave the group. Unfortunately, when only one person has all the answers, the relationship turns into a parent-child relationship. Unlearning is stunted by the capacity of the parent. Of course, a child seldom seeks what the parent wants to teach; they are looking for their own path. So it is with students who appoint themselves school masters. They are trying to convince others to follow their path of learning to affirm they have the correct lesson. This is our ego mind putting a mirror in front of us so we can learn to see differently. These lecturers reflect the authority problem in our own mind: deciding which voice to listen to, the ego or the Spiritual Eye. When you give the problem over to the Spiritual Eye for healing, it will go away.

When a study group's students, as equals, open themselves to questioning and unlearning, a higher intelligence teaches the group as a whole and everyone shares in the bounty. This is the process of forming a "Circle for Forgiveness." It opens a portal in our unconsciousness mind to allow God's love to flow into our conscious awareness. I know a higher intelligence teaches every class and its methods and techniques.

Additional directions and suggestion from Bill Thetford and Helen Schucman have come to light in recent years. They suggest ways to study "ACIM," Indicating learning among equals is the very method the Scribes intended. Lecturing is just one form of teaching, but reading together causes unlearning. Our Teacher is internal and individual to each student, and that is who you want to find: your internal teacher. The answers are within.

Tape Groups, Lecturers and Classes

Some classes wish to listen to tapes of other lecturers sharing their knowledge. I have always found it a distraction to listen to a tape while in a group. The rhythms created by reading, discussing, questioning and reading again are broken. Tape study groups have their purpose and place, but "ACIM" assures us its purpose is help each of us find this internal Teacher to guide our lessons. This is a delicate process, and it will emerge and become obvious to us through trial and error. Listening to tapes or having one person lead the discussion are excellent learning methods, but my purpose is to share with you the process given our study group in our 10-year unlearning experience. The challenge is to become willing to allow the clutter and obstacles that prevent us from following directions. The solution is how we allow the Spiritual Eye's grace to flow across these obstacles we have created. We have solved the riddle when we stop restricting the experience of God's Love.

Groups Have Beginnings and Ends

I have found most groups tend to last for a finite period of time, serving their purpose and then going away. Do not be concerned if you have months or even years of intense group participation, only to see interest and attendance dwindle before the group dissipates. I am convinced this is a part of the Plan. Groups form and perform for specific purposes – but disappear when the purpose no longer exists. It is not failure. You will better understand why as I introduce you to members of our study group. We were together for more than eight years, a consistent group of regulars and others who came and went. We noticed our regulars were having major changes in their lives. Many had life goals they expressed in our group, and they began to unfold before us on a weekly basis.

There was Rolf from Switzerland, a well-traveled and educated engineer who found his way to Dallas. When I first met Rolf, he was unemployed and buying small ownership interests in producing oil wells with credit cards. I thought he was crazy. Crude oil prices were at a low. I remember Rolf best for quoting "*ACIM*" in his heavy Swiss accent, "I need do nussing (nothing)." His investments proved to be wise ones. Rolf bought a beach house on the U.S. Virgin islands, and I am sure his credit card investments now bring him great returns.

Judy was our facilitator. She was divorced and lived alone. During the last year of our group meetings, Judy reconnected with her high school sweetheart. He owned an RV, so she quit her job at a school and joined him for many travels across the United States.

Sherry owned a very successful bakery and sandwich shop in a nearby town. She would get up each morning at 5 a.m. to begin the day's cooking. We always heard horror stories around Thanksgiving about the 600 pumpkin pies ordered for delivery on the same day. Sherry's dream was to move to the Oregon coast. Eventually, she sold her business and headed west.

Gerard was a software engineer for a major company in Dallas. He, too, wanted to live on the West Coast. Despite much trepidation about relocating, he eventually followed the setting sun. Somewhere near Bakersfield, California, he decided to go to San Diego. I had dinner with Gerard recently, and he loves San Diego.

Diane wanted to move to Boulder, Colorado, and she did. William worked at the convention center and was looking for a career change, and found one. He would always come in late to tell us of his stressful work day. We would listen to him for as long as we could, then someone would suggest we read the next paragraph. As you would suspect, answers to the day's troubles would follow, and we would laugh knowingly.

Not everyone moved away. Barbara still lives in Dallas and volunteered her skills to edit my writing. Pat, a high school counselor, still teaches. As you can imagine, many others came and went over the years. Not everyone was happy or had wealthy endings. We had a cancer patient who became extremely irritated at our lengthy discussions. She had lost all of her hair to chemotherapy and was insistent we read through the Text, as her time was limited. "ACIM's" position is that healing is of the mind, and not necessarily of the body; physical healing and recovery doesn't always take place, as the group came to discover.

Chuck was a bright young man of 35 when he first attended our classes. As his physical appearance deteriorated, it became obvious he had a serious disease. Chuck eventually identified the sickness as AIDS, but repeatedly refused to take medication. He eventually died of the illness. I can only assume he consciously chose this path. His humility in accepting his inevitable fate was courageous. But this is the paradox: I understand intellectually that death of the body is not our end in reality, but emotionally, I have a huge investment in proving the body is real and it is my only identity.

Medicine as Magic

The Course suggests therapy and medicine are forms of magic which change our physical and mental nature. Magic is the ability to change things we have made with our ego thought system – a definition unique to "ACIM." We are not told to avoid therapy and medicine, but to understand and distinguish the capabilities of mental versus physical healing. Other than extending the hand of friendship and a loving offer of forgiveness, we can do nothing more. Our purpose is to heal our own mind and to accept the Atonement for ourselves.

As Chuck passed, our group numbers continued to dwindle until one night, Judy and I sat looking at just each other. I knew the class had come to an end, and felt a great deal of sadness. Our purpose together as a group had been completed. I will rely on Longfellow words from *The Day is Done* to convey my feelings:

> *And the night shall be filled with music,*
> *And the cares, that infest the day,*
> *Shall fold their tents, like the Arabs,*
> *And as silently steal away.*

The Rules for Decision

"*ACIM*'s" published edition's Chapter 30 is titled, "The New Beginnings." It is an extremely important chapter because the first section contains the "Rules for Decision" It suggests we must learn to question every problem when it arises, for there is a reason we have chosen to experience a perceived dilemma. We have made a decision with our egos and misunderstood what we are perceiving as a problem, because we have listened to the wrong voice in our mind – the ego.

The sadness I experiencing when our class ended was a part of the grieving process over the end of such a beautiful experience. My ego wanted to see it as a failure. It told me we should have multitudes standing in line to join our group because we had baskets of loaves and fishes to pass out. Alas, it was not true. Our relationships had been transformed from special to holy relationships. The group's lessons had ended and our members had folded their tents and slipped away to new experiences and lessons. In fact, we were a complete success. It was my misperception but when corrected, it brought peace and a deep sense of joyful accomplishment. A failure was now seen as triumph.

A Haven in Times of Trouble

I sorely miss the group's 10 years of companionship and support. It was a relief and haven in troubled times; I always found answers to life's difficult problems. Because our church facility was near a major Dallas highway, some joined our group purely by mistake. It was not unusual for someone to wander in off the street, asking for money, food or prayer. We always invited them to join us and read the Course. Occasionally, some did.

The church decided to make its facilities available to other religious groups during weekdays as a means of community outreach. We had several start-up churches that occupied the sanctuary on Tuesday nights while we read in the library. A metaphysical group burned incense and mediated. A traveling guru with long hair passed through; we suspected he had a Jesus Complex – non-judgmental suspicion, of course. Above all, I remember the Pentecostal church group with exclusively black members. When their music began, our reading stopped. I believe all these experiences opened my mind to the concept that spiritual healing takes many forms and many avenues. It always seemed as we read about miracles and healing of the mind, something similar was going on down the hall in a different format.

More than once I had to swallow my intellectual arrogance and realize that an "act of love" is always given at a level of understanding for which the "call for love" can be received. I need medication – the magic – for some illnesses. I can accomplish healing with that level of understanding. Almost certainly, when I am ready to ask, "What is this for? I don't like what I am experiencing," I get an answer. The malady will have served its purpose and many times, it goes away.

Modern-Day Scribes and Pharisees

After the Tuesday night group disbanded, a Sunday morning group appeared. This class facilitated the new look at the Book of Revelation. The group still meets today but at its peak attendance, it was the most accomplished and informed class in one location. Most of the students had been studying for more than 20 years. There was Arthur and Peter, who had frequently attended Kenneth Wapnick's classes in Roscoe, N.Y. They are gadflies, always questioning presented concepts and acting as the ego's advocate. If you listen closely to some of Dr. Wapnick's taped sessions, you might hear Arthur's relentless questioning. He takes pride in being referred to as the tiny worm in the dust and as having no significance. Arthur, a Jew, always wanted to know why he should believe in the Holy Spirit. Both he and Peter are dear friend and wonderful teachers.

Duane and Sissy was a delightful couple who were studying Edgar Cayce's works when "*ACIM*" was first introduced. They were friends with Hugh Lynn Cayce, who suggested to Dr. Schucman and Dr. Thetford there were "two voices" dictating the Course's message.

Duane and Sissy met Thetford as other significant players in *"ACIM's"* early beginnings and publishing.

Many guests insisted on lecturing us for two hours, directing our readings to follow their lectures or playing tapes, with starts and stops like a traffic light. This created a saw-tooth rhythm and confusion but fortunately, Arthur would throw a wrench into the spokes and pull us back to the Text with a Holy Instant. But there were intense times, also.

Many of the original members have now passed on. It was a joy to see them face sickness and death with a sense of calm and reassurance, with the strength of the Course's Elder Brother. He redefines crucifixion so that our focuse is on resurrection and not death. Fortunately, new members continue to arrive and the group continues reading.

We must enjoy this time God has put us together, for what God has joined for a holy purpose, no man can tear asunder. These relationships are welded with bonds of a healing love. They have no opposition and a singular purpose: to speed us on the pathway home to an awareness of life eternal.

Come, I Will Make you Fishers of Men

I must tell you about my son. When he was 12 years old, his best friends moved away. They were twin brothers, which mean he lost two play companions. One summer morning when he was in a particular funk over the lost playmates, I suggested we go fishing. His previous experience with fishing was with my father at farm ponds, which was like fishing in a barrel. Every cast got a fish. Our few Texas fishing attempts had resulted in empty hooks and his interest level fell rapidly. With a promise of success, he finally agreed to fish in Oklahoma.

I packed the essentials: a cooler, box of fried chicken, Game Boy, fly fishing bags, waders, headphones, etc. My son slept in the back of our old SUV until we arrived at Blue River in Southern Oklahoma, a trout fishing stream usually stocked in the winter. Unfortunately, we arrived during the summer. Our attempts to catch fish were futile. It was hot and only mosquitoes were biting.

When all else fails, change bait. Off we went to the local bait store seeking comfort, advice and a box of worms. Explaining my dilemma to the attendant, he suggested: "Well take your son to the National Hatchery just down the road. It's a great place to fish!" A hatchery! An oasis in the wilderness!

As we crossed the bridge to the hatchery, the grounds crews were finishing their yard work. The lawn, now neatly trimmed, was sitting next to a rippling spring-fed stream overhung with live oaks that formed a canopy above cool, clear waters. The crew welcomed us with open arms and helped us unload our gear. What a setting – and nobody else around!

After eating our fried chicken, we put on waders and entered the water with great anticipation. This was my son's first attempt at fly fishing. If you have ever had this experience, then you know about the tangled mess that followed. My son waded out until he was chest deep, thrashing the water with his fly rod. This sent a strong message to any nearby fish: beware, we are on the stalk.

It didn't take long, after about 15 minutes of intense activity, I heard a sigh of relief and as small voice come across the water, "This is sweet!" His sorrow and cares folded their tents and slipped away. They, too, were Arabs in the night. I could not explain what he would experience or what would happen when he went fishing. It was my past experiences fishing with my father that promised a change of mind. Because of this, I knew what would happen when he got in the water. And so it did. We went swimming together and had a great time playing in the stream. I contend playing in the water is the real purpose of every fisherman.

A Circle of Forgiveness will yield the same relief from fear, anxiety and the day's frustrations. When we join together with others in a Holy purpose, to unlearn, miraculous things happen. We will find relief as specific answers to life's complex problems present themselves through simple reading and then shared with fellow students. The answers will not only be specific to the immediate application, but also heal the underlying relationships from which they continually arise. When these relationships are cured at the source, fear and anxiety become less frequent. When they do return, you can recall the memory of healing. Like wade fishing, just walk right in the water and experience the refreshing effects of sharing your woes and triumphs.

It will transform your life, giving a new meaning to "fishers of men." The experience of reading and discussing *"ACIM"* awakens you to the internal Teacher – which is the Course's purpose.

Only Suggested Guidelines for a Circle of Forgiveness

I have written much about *"ACIM's"* benefits and the experiences others have gained from reading in groups or by themselves. Just as true revelation cannot be expressed in words comprehensible to others, neither can the experience of Peace of Mind and happiness. It must be an experience undertaken with free will for mutual learning. The teacher is really the student. When ready, I know teachers will appear; it happens for each of us. As we undertake our place in God's Plan of Atonement, we will learn the lessons of forgiveness and how to perform miracles. Again, miracles are a change in our mind, in time. We are separated only in time, and time as we know it is drawing to an end.

My suggestions for facilitating study groups are based on my experience. Nothing is cast in stone. When you decide to undertake your place in God's Plan of Salvation, whatever is necessary will be given to you. Likewise, whoever is called to join with you will find you. Do not engage in tribulation. Your internal Teacher will direct you to the students from which you will learn. Remember, the students are your teachers. You are engaged in an unlearning process known as the Great Crusade. Relax, rejoice and be glad, for you have nothing but happiness and joy on the road ahead.

Forgiveness in A Circle

On a closing note, let me tell you how the phrase, "Circle of Forgiveness," came into my conscious awareness. January 15, 2005, was the first shopping day for the Chinese New Year – still three weeks off – in Singapore. Like our Christmas, the Chinese New Year is a time of family renewal, good food, gift giving and great celebrations. This January 15th reminded me of the day after Thanksgiving here in the U.S. Chinatown's streets were packed with shoppers and bargain hunters searching for cakes, candles and other specific gifts. I was soaking in the excitement when I came upon a "chop shop." A chop is a stone carving used for signing one's name, similar to an official seal. Artists place their chops on works of art. Certain transactions in

China and Southeast Asia cannot be completed without the chop's red-ink stamp on documents. It is a powerful symbol, not unlike a professional seal.

I decided I needed a chop with my name, but while translating my named to be carved in stone, the thought occurred to make the chop into a symbol for "circle of forgiveness." Why not in Chinese characters? I may never know why, but I have learned to follow intuition at times. The design and transactions were handled by two women who were anxious to fill my request. However, this simple process took on new proportions. No one knew how to translate circle into a Chinese character and then combine it with forgiveness.

I was expecting two Chinese characters side by side reading "circle" and "forgiveness." It took an hour of phone calls to owners and translators, who chattered in Cantonese as they determined the best way to convey the message. What emerged was a combination of the characters for forgiveness placed inside a circle. It translates as "circle of forgiveness" or "forgiveness in a circle," (see above) though a circle is not a traditional Chinese character. These wonderful women wasted no time finishing the project. After two confirming phone calls with local linguists, they were convinced the translation was correct. What followed was most fascinating. The two shop keepers begin to loudly chant the phrase in English such that it filled the street in front of the booth, attracting attention from passers-by. They would not stop. "Circle of Forgiveness! Circle of Forgiveness!" It struck a chord. For the women, it was a feeling of accomplishment beyond their normal duties of engraving names on chops. They had created a "Circle of Forgiveness."

More recently, when I ask someone who understands Chinese characters to translate the image, they usually place their hand over their heart and then motion their hand toward me and say, "I forgive you." As you will remember from our previous discussions, forgiveness in *"ACIM"* is not about forgiving acts done or not done. Forgiveness, in this context, is forgiving others for our misperceptions about being physical bodies and not spiritual beings. We should ask forgiveness for our misidentification. Hence, "I forgive myself by acknowledging the Christ in you!"

The finished chop was placed in a quaint wooden box to prevent damage and I proceeded on my way. It was a significant experience for me, but it must have struck a deep resonance with the two women, the engraver and the passers-by, based on the excitement and chanting. It involved six people who, working in unison, formatted a concept into a verbal and visual expression heretofore unexpressed. A "Circle of Forgiveness" became a graven image in stone, in characters used by more than a billion people. Not a bad day's work for the two women. They had expressed the beauty that takes place with forgiveness in a circle.

According to a miracle's definition, what transpired in the chop shop was an out-of-pattern sequence that moved outside of space and time. Forgiveness' release was profound. As those two women begin to shout and chant, "Circle of Forgiveness! Circle of Forgiveness!" a tremendous joy was released, followed by great celebration. When two or more come together for a holy purpose, miraculous things happen. Forgiveness had been graven in stone. The blessing of its circle is inclusive of everyone.

The universe responded accordingly. Later that night, Singapore's Chinatown was packed with visitors and celebration. What transpired was the world's largest fireworks display, celebrating the beginning of the Chinese New Year – and just maybe, another miraculous event that happened that very day. While some might suggest the fireworks are a planned annual event, you and I know differently! At least believing this it is a pleasing to my ego.

Timelessness Waits on Time

Timelessness is another means of expressing Heaven, where there is no time. Imagine that our experience of time is nothing more than a great circle returning to the beginning point at each moment, in time. This is like the loops around a daisy's petals. These loops, in time, are shortening as more awaken to the awareness of the Christ-Self in each mind. With the beauty and symmetry of a yellow and white daisy, all petals are connected to the center. The time it takes us to complete the loop between beginnings and end is accelerating. In fact, we never left the beginning except in the world of time and in our ego minds.

This section now comes to a close, as does our obsession with time. The ending of time need not be horrific or catastrophic. It will be a gentle closing – as will the Second Coming of Christ – into our conscious awareness. The world as we know it "will disappear," but that means only our perception of the material world will change. How will the world in which we live and breathe formulate after the Second Coming? We do not know. If anyone truly knew the nature of Heaven, he would have told us all by now. We do know that our part is performing miracles through forgiveness that moves us to Heaven's Gate. In time, God will take the final step for us into Heaven. This is a promise from "*ACIM.*" There we have complete knowledge of our Christ being, experiencing happiness and joy, however that may be defined.

"All things we have made to measure time will disappear. When they no longer have a use, they will return no more. Only the eternal, our Spirit, will remain in timelessness where it now resides; where it has always been. Our Christ-Self lives in timelessness while our ego-self waits in time, planning frantic activities to sustain our existence. But time is coming to an end." "A Course in Miracles"

The End of Time

Nothing in the world must change,

Nothing is defined for the purpose given.

But how lovely the world,

When forgiveness is our purpose.

How beautiful is this universe,

When we are free from fear.

How glorious is our life,

As we choose happiness.

Filled with God's blessing,

Instead of a dream of death.

And what a joy it is to dwell,

If for only a moment,

In such a happy place;

A world of forgiveness.

Nor will it be forgotten,

For in a little while,

Timelessness comes quietly,

To take the place of time.

For the end of time,

Was written in the stars.

Long ago, was it set in Heaven.

Held with a shinning Ray,

Safe within Eternity,

Through all time as well.

And it holds still:

Unchanged,

Unchanging,

Unchangeable.

We have lost our way,

He has found it.

Let us bid Him welcome,

Him who has returned!

Let us celebrate salvation,

And the end of what we made.

The morning star of a new day,

Welcomes God, His Son,

And the end of time.

(Excerpts from "ACIM")

Epilogue

This publication's first edition contained a Section II which included the first four chapters of *"A Course in Miracles"* for personal study and use as a Text for those who chose to facilitate and read in a "Circle of Forgiveness." These chapters used the term Spiritual Eye rather than Holy Spirit. They contained references to the "Celestial Speed–Up" and many other subjects not in the current published editions.

Since that time, several previous editions of *"ACIM"* have been released, shedding considerable light on the Scribe's notes and experiences in first publishing the Text. Section II containing the first four chapters that had been deleted from the second edition.

If you decide to start a study group, you will be able to find copies of the many editions which are now in publication. The message remains the same and I am sure you will be guided in the right direction, if you ask your Internal Teacher.

You now join with thousands of others in this Great Crusade. The "Celestial Speed–Up" propels us toward the End of Time, where God patiently stands awaiting our arrival with the gifts of happiness and eternal peace of mind. The Second Coming has begun. As we each take our part in God's Plan of Atonement, we enter timelessness together.

> *"Bring all of your stores into the storehouse so that there may be food in my house and, prove me, sayeth the Lord, if I will not pour forth a blessing, so great, that you cannot receive it all."*

> *Malachi 3:10*

Selected Bibliography

Edinger MD, Edward F., *Archetype of the Apocalypse*, Open Court Press, PO Box 300, Peru, Illinois 61354. 1999.

Edinger MD, Edward F., *Ego and Archetype*, Shambhala, 800 Mass Ave, Boston 02115, 1972.

Hoeller, Stephan A., *The Gnostic Jung*, Theosophical Pub. House, Wheaton, Ill, 1982.

Jenkins, Jerry B., *Left Behind Series*, http://en.wikipedia.org/wiki/Jerry B. Jenkins, &/Left Behind # Plot summary.

Jung, C. G., *Answer to Job*, Translated by RFC Hull, Princeton Univ. Press, 1973.

Jung, C. G., *Memories, Dreams, Reflections*, Vintage Books, New York, 1961.

Scofield's Reference Bible, excerpts courtesy, http://en.wikipedia.org/wiki/Scofield_Reference_Bible

Sharp, Daryl, *Jung Lexicon A Primer in Terms and Concepts*, Inner City Books, 1991

Spiegel MD, David , *Comments on Dissociation*: http://pstlab.stanford.edu/dissoc.html:

Wapnick PhD., Kenneth, *THE EARLY MANUSCRIPT OF "A COURSE IN MIRACLES" GIVEN TO HUGH LYNN CAYCE,* from notes by Kenneth Wapnick, Ph.D. website and also copyright 1992 by the Foundation for A Course in Miracles®

Wapnick PhD, Kenneth*, Absence From Felicity*, The Story of Helen Schucman and Her Scribing of A Course in Miracles, copyright 1991, Foundation for A Course in Miracles.

The New American Bible, Introduction to Revelations,
http://www.nccbuscc.org/nab/bible/revelation/intro.htm

The Jerusalem Bible, copyright 1968, Darton, Longman & Todd Ltd
and Doubleday & Company, Inc.

A Course in Miracles, copyright vacated, Penguin Group, 1973

Tao Te Ching, Vintage, by Gia-Fu Cheng and Jane English, Vintage
Books, 1972

Printed in the United States
By Bookmasters